PARTY AND POLITICAL OPPOSITION IN REVOLUTIONARY AMERICA

Editor: Patricia U. Bonomi

THE SLEEPY HOLLOW PRESS

SLEEPY HOLLOW RESTORATIONS
TARRYTOWN • NEW YORK

Library of Congress Cataloging in Publication Data
Main entry under title:

Party and political opposition in Revolutionary America.

Includes bibliographical references and index.
1. Political parties--United States--History--Addresses,
essays, lectures. 2. United States--Politics and government--
Revolution, 1775–1783--Addresses, essays, lectures. 3. Op-
position (Political science)--Addresses, essays, lectures.
I. Bonomi, Patricia U.
JK2260.P37   324.2732   80-13480
ISBN 0-912882-39-5

First Printing

For information, address the publisher:

The Sleepy Hollow Press
Sleepy Hollow Restorations, Inc.
150 White Plains Road
Tarrytown, New York 10591

ISBN 0-912882-39-5
Library of Congress Catalog Card Number 80-13480

Manufactured in the United States of America

CONTENTS

Introduction   v
  Patricia U. Bonomi
Civil Wars, Revolutions, and Political Parties   1
  J.G.A. Pocock
Religion and Politics in Revolutionary New England:
Natural Rights Reconsidered   13
  Stephen Botein
The Legal and Religious Context of
Natural Rights Theory: A Comment   35
  Stanley N. Katz
The Pattern of Factional Development in Pennsylvania,
New York, and Massachusetts, 1682-1776   43
  Marc Egnal
Empire and Faction: A Comment   61
  Alison Gilbert Olson
"Greedy Party Work": The South Carolina
Election of 1768   70
  David R. Chesnutt
Another View of the South Carolina Election of 1768
and the Regulators: A Comment   87
  Joseph A. Ernst
Parties and the Transformation of the Constitutional
Idea in Revolutionary Pennsylvania   98
  George Dargo
Constitutional Formalism or the Politics of Virtue?:
A Comment   115
  Stephen E. Patterson
Notes   119
Contributors   149
Index   151

INTRODUCTION

The Bicentennial of the American Revolution provided many an occasion for reassessments of the early American experience. One of these was the "Conference on Party and Faction in Revolutionary America" sponsored by Sleepy Hollow Restorations at Tarrytown, New York, whose purpose was to examine the role of parties and formed oppositions in the Revolutionary era and to suggest new and productive approaches to the study of Revolutionary politics. The essays that appear in this volume are revised and expanded versions of the conference papers, and with the exception of J.G.A. Pocock's contribution, which was originally offered as a dinner address, each is followed by a comment, also revised and enlarged since the original presentation.

Any discussion of factions and parties[1] in the Revolutionary era is inevitably linked to the continuing debate among historians about the general character of eighteenth-century American society. For to suggest what a people fought over implies an interpretation of the values of their society, and calls attention to those principles, or material goals, or symbols of power and status they appear to have cherished most. Even to make an assessment of the amount of factional conflict involves a judgment on the significance of the Revolution as a pivotal event. For not everyone agrees on whether it is more accurate to portray Revolutionary Americans as a people discovering unity and nationhood in a set of political and moral principles so compelling as to transcend their many cultural and economic differences, or to portray them as a culturally fragmented and contentious people who subdued their divisive impulses only long enough to wrest independence from Great Britain and then immediately resumed their factious ways. Further differences of interpretation arise over the question of how Americans' provincial experience with opposition politics may have shaped their attitudes and behavior toward England as the Revolutionary crisis deepened.

Historians have been writing about colonial parties since at least the early twentieth century, and while interpretations vary, most agree that parties were more likely to form in the north than in the south, and that episodes of factional strife alternated with periods of political calm. But whereas the official expectations of that age of oligarchy pointed to a restrained, decorous, and relatively equable political style, and since the facts were frequently otherwise, we find our interest again and again attracted to the spasmodic turbulence of provincial politics and its tendency to spin out of control. And this leads to questions about the basis of faction itself. What issues or contending interests led people to separate into rival groups? Were there continuities over time and across provincial boundaries that form a larger pattern of explanation? And what were the implications of this formative period for the long-term habits of American political life?

Over the years historians have explored many levels of the eighteenth-century American experience in order to see more clearly into our early political culture. The first generation of scholars to take a specific interest in colonial parties proceeded with confidence to identify the forces in contention as those of *demos* and *aristos*. This view was subsequently challenged by those who preferred to emphasize the comparatively broad base upon which colonial politics rested, or who were impressed by the corporate integrity of community life in the provinces. But this more inclusive and unitary interpretation had always to be balanced against the deferential norms of eighteenth-century public life, and whatever temptation there may have been to associate an emergently popular style of colonial politics with "democracy" was tempered by the obvious unsuitability of using a modern political vocabulary to describe an essentially pre-modern society.[2] On the other hand, the usefulness of deference itself as a comprehensive principle of explanation was limited by the apparent unwillingness of so many provincials to stay in their place, as the commotions caused by Paxton Boys, land rioters, and urban crowds seemed to show a decline of deference that at times verged on insolence.

As these studies of political behavior went forward, another line of investigation was taking a closer look at political structure. The "imperial" historians had laid the groundwork for it in their multi-volume works on the formal institutions of government. More recently, however, interest has been drawn to the informal side of provincial and imperial politics. The mechanisms by which colonial assemblies converted themselves into little parliaments have been more fully discerned, revealing both the transitional and the innovative aspects of American political development. The erosion of executive authority and the resultant disparity between the powers formally assigned to governors and those actually at their disposal has been noted. As royal executives bartered away some of their control over patronage, "influence" declined as a means of managing colonial politicians; meanwhile, colonials were developing their own informal channels of political access, through English business associates, relatives, and agents. The absence of an aristocratic order to provide a stable center in a mixed constitutional system has also been noted; likewise the anomaly of a parvenu leadership for which one qualified primarily through a talent for making money.[3] By exposing the inner workings of Anglo-American politics, these studies have illuminated the increasing disjunction between formal English structures of government and the realities of colonial political practice. Moreover, the colonists' growing uncertainty about the power whereby their affairs were being regulated — how that power was in fact used, how it could or should be restrained, and how they ought to think about these questions — contributed directly, it has been suggested, to the volatility and "milling factionalism" that marked the final decades of provincial politics.[4]

Even in their awareness of the unstable condition of colonial politics, students of political structure have usually depicted factional divisions as random and ephemeral rather than rooted in social or economic discontents.[5] Recent work by social historians, however, has aroused new interest in the specific sources of grievance and tension in early American society. Whether our belated recognition that some eighteenth-century Americans were weak or poor or the victims of social inequities, or that economic fortunes could fall as well as rise, will lead in turn to a refurbishing of the class theory of colonial parties remains to be seen. So far, the outlines of a "moral economy" that might link class consciousness to ideology remain indistinct. One immediate result of this work, however, has been to give added weight to conflict as a significant theme in colonial culture.[6]

If a coherent explanation for political conflict continues to elude us, something may yet be gained from a study of the symptoms. Thus it has been suggested, by myself and others, that the high incidence of factionalism, irrespective of its possible causes or social basis, can itself tell us something of a patterned nature not only about the politics of the time but even about our entire subsequent political development. Two aspects of this problem bear mentioning here. For one, the proliferation of faction in socially heterogeneous provinces — the middle colonies, to be sure, but also in such places as Rhode Island, Maryland, and North Carolina — suggests a relationship between party and cultural diversity. Religious, ethnic, and economic subgroups emerged as collective entities in those colonies, and in a number of places they began to make themselves felt as "self-interest groups."[7] This factious activity weighed heavily, however, on the eighteenth-century political mind, for colonists were aware at some level of consciousness that a slippage was developing within their own values — between the negative value of "party" and their own recurrent involvement in party activities. Driven to reconcile principles with practice, some colonists experimented with what we would today call an interest-group theory of politics, while others went so far as to hint that parties might make a positive contribution to the preservation of liberty by serving as a device for checking power in the state.[8] Moreover, the most precocious testing of these thoughts occurred in colonies where interests were most diverse and party

viii

activity most advanced. The party impulse was necessarily repressed, to be sure, during the War for Independence and the early years of nation-building, when unity was the first essential of existence. But when it re-emerged in the nineteenth century — far in advance of similar developments in other western countries — the party idea gained legitimacy first in those parts of the new nation where the struggles of an earlier time had left a deposit of experience upon which to build.

Such, then, are some of the ways in which historians have viewed parties and factions in provincial America since they first became a subject of explicit interest in the early twentieth century. The contributors to this book are familiar with this literature, though they have in no way been confined by it. Their essays and commentary have not only absorbed previous categories of interpretation, they have in a number of instances transcended them. Out of this work, we venture to hope, may come new categories, new themes, new light.

The discussion opens on the elevated plane offered by J.G.A. Pocock's comparison of English and American political structures in the seventeenth and eighteenth centuries. Starting from a common heritage of medieval parliamentarianism, the two societies had diverged sharply by 1776, with England retaining and building upon the parliamentary model while Americans reached back to the classical ideal of separation and balance of powers in forming their democratic republic. Professor Pocock suggests that this divergence may have been caused in part by differences in the way political energy was mobilized in each society and directed from local to national objects. While the relationships of influence — the "connexions" — of English politics created a symbiosis between Parliament and shire, court and country, the oligarchies of provincial America were never able to duplicate the power networks of the English counties or to compete effectively with them. Being outsiders, the Americans felt much freer to criticize the English political system, and finally to break sharply from it.

Stephen Botein is likewise concerned with a large political theme as he examines how Americans, and particularly New Englanders, justified their opposition to British policies in the Revolutionary era. Professor Botein argues persuasively that natural rights theory should be restored to a prominent place as an influential component of Revolutionary thought. The legal and constitutional emphasis that typifies the New Englanders' Revolutionary vocabulary was, he believes, the logical outgrowth of a religious culture that for over a century had stressed the contractual character of the relationship between people and minister, and between citizen and authority. Whether in the form of Scripturally-based "Christian rights," as expounded by the traditionalist clergy, or in the "natural law" terms emphasized by rationalist eighteenth-century ministers, natural rights philosophy became such a familiar part of the New Englanders' social and political experience that it may well have provided "the most broadly popular constitutional vocabulary" for their Revolutionary understanding. In his comment, Stanley Katz considers the legal and religious setting from which natural rights theory emerged.

A question that has long intrigued students of colonial politics is whether any significant connections can be drawn between the political factions of provincial America and the colonists' division into Patriot and Loyalist at the time of the Revolution. After reviewing the main features of factional conflict in Pennsylvania, New York, and Massachusetts, especially from 1740 to the Revolution, Marc Egnal discerns a pattern which in his view provides coherence and continuity to party alignments over the thirty-five-year span. Surveying emergent attitudes toward territorial aggrandizement, imperial regulation, currency policies, and New World nationalism, Professor Egnal sees the people of those three colonies dividing into "expansionists" and "non-expansionists," the one tending to become Patriots, the other being more likely to remain loyal to England. Alison Gilbert Olson's commentary examines Mr. Egnal's thesis in a larger imperial framework.

The southern colonies pose a different sort of problem. The emergence of cohesive leadership elites in eighteenth-century Virginia, South Carolina, and Georgia led to an apparent *absence* of factional tension — a condition so unusual in colonial America as itself to call for an explanation. As David Chesnutt's study of the South

Carolina assembly election of 1768 shows, restive interest groups —
in this case the backcountry legislators and the Charleston mechanics
— which might have provided the materials for party conflict were
clearly present in South Carolina by the 1760's. Yet owing to the
structures of power in the colony, the access to land and other
resources, and the gentry's long experience in accommodating
disparate interests, the flash point was never reached. South Carolinians had more than adequate resources for subduing internal conflicts
and restoring a united political front. The commentator, Joseph
Ernst, offers a reconsideration of the Regulators' role in the election
of 1768, and finds real sources of division in South Carolina.

The indulgent attitude shown in a number of colonies toward partisan activity before the Revolution stands in sharp contrast to the
universal rejection of parties by American political theorists after
1776. In the final essay, George Dargo observes that even in such a
place as Pennsylvania, where formed political oppositions were commonplace, no group went so far as to advocate a party "system" as an
appropriate means for checking power in the new state. The explanation, according to Professor Dargo, lies in the founders' determination to eliminate from politics all such capricious and volatile
elements as factions and parties, and to construct their new governments on "scientific" principles that were firmly fixed in written constitutions. In his comment, Stephen Patterson points to both the
ideology of republicanism and the continuing undercurrent of partisanship in the Revolutionary era as influences on the founders'
political thought.

PATRICIA U. BONOMI
New York University

Party and Political Opposition in Revolutionary America

Editor: Patricia U. Bonomi

Civil Wars, Revolutions, and Political Parties

J. G. A. Pocock

In this essay I shall not be concerned narrowly with the structure of party in colonial societies, but with the wider historical background to this question that may be furnished by comparing the development of party in England and America considered as national societies. How far party in the colonies before the Revolution may be deemed continuous with party in the early United States is for others to decide.

I shall, to begin with, review some recent changes in historiographical perspective which have affected our understanding of parties in eighteenth-century England and may be used to improve our analysis of parties in American history. I shall use the word "England" instead of "Britain" because Scotland and Ireland were still half-alien societies, imperfectly assimilated to the political styles of the dominant culture. Scotland was a dependent province where political participation was sharply limited; Ireland one where political culture of any kind had but recently struggled into semi-existence. It is a matter of some importance that several at least of the American colonies fit neither description.

We were all, I think, brought up on a potent if soporific brew of Namier-and-branch-water which tended to persuade us that at any given moment there were no parties but only connections. This term refers to a pattern of relationships between patronge-wielding families, and between them and their clients and dependents, which existed for some centuries, and in varying forms, in the political universe of the English county gentry; and the use of the term refers us equally to the existence of connection in the politics of the shire and in the politics of the House of Commons. The paradigm of connection—to simplify its use somewhat below the true level of Namierian understanding—seeks to persuade us that relationships formed in the counties tended to dominate behavior in the national assembly of Parliament. To some extent this was founded on a false dichotomy, produced in pursuit of the red herring of anti-ideologism; Namier and his followers did belong to that irreducible reductionism, endemic in the historical profession, which constantly denies that men's actions are shaped by their beliefs even where it has never been asserted that they are. In this case it had never been seriously argued by any historian I can think of that the Whig and Tory parties were alliances based on a community of beliefs; it had only been argued that beliefs did exist and were important; but nothing will satisfy the hunters of the red herring, who will simply impute to one the positions they desire to refute. The serious (if perhaps still misstated) problem raised by the paradigm of connection is that of determining how far men were divided and regrouped by political issues generated at the centers of government, how far by issues generated at the periphery and in the provinces; how far the capital may be dissolved into the grassroots, the court into the country.

The changes in historical understanding I want to review all have to do with this question, and the first of them in chronological order arises from the recent research into the character of the English Civil War of the mid-seventeenth century. A.M. Everitt has revived—I do not diminish the originality of his thinking by using this term— the concept of the county community,[1] the network of connections and alliances, affinities and consanguinities, formed by the relationships of the landholding gentry in counties and groups of counties; and he has stressed that the political consciousness of such a community might be introspective to the point where it approached or aimed at autonomy. The dominant political aim of such a community of gentry might be to protect their relationships, and even their rivalries, from interference by the central government, and this motive comes to the surface, in a great many obvious ways, under the shock of civil war.

Following Everitt there has grown up a habit of alluding to seventeenth-century England as almost a confederation of autonomous rural city-states. But, as Shakespeare so nearly wrote, this is the English, not the Polish court; not Jagellon to Jagellon succeeds, but Stuart Tudor. In his study of the Eastern Association during the Civil War, Clive Holmes[2] has shown that East Anglia, the group of counties where one of the most effective of the parliamentary armies was produced, differed from the rest of England not at all in the intensity of its fragmentary local particularisms, but rather in the efficacy with which Manchester, and later Cromwell, supported by officials whom Parliament had appointed, were able to coordinate country resources. East Anglian regional characteristics mattered only as offering handles for Parliament to grasp, and Holmes unarguably concludes that the county community, for all its stubborn and irreducible localism, can only be thought of in its relation to the central government. The Tudors, he sums up, had done their work too well. So for that matter had the Angevins and the kings of Wessex.

Holmes is telling us that court and country, even when in conflict, existed in symbiosis. I want to argue that this generalization is crucial to the history of party in England; but I also want to contend that the history of the Civil War can be reinterpreted as part of that history. In the first place, it was phenomena like those studied by Holmes which ensured that the resort to violence in seventeenth-century England was not a collapse into feudal anarchy, nor the dissolution of society into a state of nature, but that very different thing, a civil war; which may be defined as the continuation of conflict within a political system by Clausewitzian means, not uncommonly ending in the reassertion of the political system, the reinforcement of its authority, and the victory of whatever faction is most effectively associated with that authority—as Parliament won the war in 1646 and the monarchy was restored in 1660. The political system generates its own conflicts and survives them; it is herein that civil wars differ from revolutions. But in the second place, it was the ascendancy of central authority over local communities and connections which obliged Englishmen to fight one another in civil war, when most of them were profoundly reluctant to do so. A truncated Parliament at Westminster and a peripatetic court moving from York to Oxford could, by sending out commissioners with writs of array, oblige county communities to take up arms against one another, or themselves to divide into warring factions. They were intensely and

bitterly unwilling to fight each other; they applied braking devices
and sabotage to the war machinery in every way they could think of;[3]
but they could deny the authority of neither of the contending halves
of government, and neutrality, though it was attempted, was no more
possible for Norfolk in 1642 than for Kentucky 220 years later. Such,
again, is the nature of civil war.

I want next to argue that this polarization of unwilling Englishmen
into Royalists and Parliamentarians ranks among the phenomena of
the history of party inasmuch as it is the first post-medieval example
of their division into groups, contending on a national stage, by the effective exportation from the center of government of issues which
caught up and transcended the world of county community and connection. The connections were still there and profoundly affected
men's actions, but the issues provided the context into which they
would not avoid responding. It is of course obvious that Parliamentarians and Royalists differ from Gilbert and Sullivan's Liberals and
Conservatives to the very considerable extent to which a civil war dif-
fers from a two-party system; but exactly how wide is that difference
and what are the ways across it?

Civil war, I have argued, is the continuation of conflict within a
political system by what Clausewitzians call "other means." It can
with plausibility be argued that what one might be tempted to call
England's first party system—the conflicts of Whig and Tory which
we trace from the reign of Charles II to that of George I—was a continuation of civil war by other means. This does not mean crudely
that Tories and Whigs were the direct heirs of Royalists and
Parliamentarians; it means in the first place that whenever, from
1678 to 1714, political conflicts at the center came to involve the succession to the throne, they raised questions of basic legitimacy to
which the gentry in their communities, and the rest of political
England, instantly responded. This response was based on an in-
grained conviction that issues of this kind could make them fight one
another a second time—in the language of 1680, "forty-one is come
again"—unless they took steps to see that this did not happen. In
1680 and 1681 they rallied to the Crown; in 1688 and 1714 to Parliament. Between the two latter dates we find a party conflict in which

the symbolography of Whig and Tory involved less the legitimacy of the Glorious Revolution itself than a conflict between two different ways of legitimating it; and since this entailed conflict between methods of determining the succession, Whigs and Tories were aware that they might have to fight one another if they were not careful. The legitimation of a revolution is a dangerous matter when there are two understandings of what the revolution has been about. I see analogies here between Whigs and Tories in the 1690's and Federalists and Republicans a hundred years later, and I suggest that both first party systems had to do with potentially delegitimating issues.

This is why—to turn to the second paradigm shift in historiography which I want to discuss—R.R. Walcott's attempt to "Namierize" the politics of Anne's reign was upset by J.H. Plumb, Geoffrey Holmes, and W.A. Speck,[4] who succeeded in showing that party conflict was intense throughout the constituencies and transcended the politics of connection in point of both ideology and organization. It was not that connections ceased to be there or to engross men's energies and attention; the point is rather that in the wake of the Glorious Revolution connection was dealing with something bigger than itself, and with divisive issues, exported to the counties, some of which could lead to civil war. It is therefore not surprising to find both an intensification of party conflict in the constituencies and a determination to liquidate conflict before any flash point could be reached.

If—to use the terminology of the historians I have mentioned—"the rage of party" was a modification of civil war by transmuting it into parliamentary conflict, "the growth of oligarchy," which rather rapidly followed the crisis of 1714, was an equivalent to the Restoration of 1660, a deliberate de-intensification of politics grown too dangerous and expensive. By the Septennial Act in Parliament, by a series of *pactes de famille* in county and borough, the gentry saw to it that political conflict should be limited in frequency and intensity, and that this damping down should apply to both the centers of power and the provincial communities. The growth of oligarchy ushered in the "Age of Namier," those partyless decades of the mid-century in which connection seemed to have reasserted its primacy in politics. But Plumb's analysis, which I follow here, leaves no doubt that, as

the growth of oligarchy followed the rage of party, the primacy of connection was not the simple reflection of a sociological fact, but a
deliberate, sustained, successful yet precarious conservative reaction.
The connections had come to town, and to court, not because the
country was at peace but to keep it so.

The determination to repress the growth of divisive issues like that
of succession is of course only one of the motives behind the growth of
oligarchy. Plumb shows clearly that the enlargement of the electorate
and the costs of local political competition were proving as disturbing
to the gentry as the intensification of party antagonism, and the
reassertion of connection politics in Parliament and uncontested elections in the constituencies operated as remedies to both kinds of
malfunction. But the conflict of Whig and Tory, which was brought to
an end soon after 1714, was also the conflict of court and country, and
the ferocity of politics during the four last years of Queen Anne was
additionally a rebellion of country gentry against what they saw as
domination by a "monied interest," its managerial politics, and expensive wars.[5] The Tories failed to erect a permanent governing party
on the basis of this rebellion, and we have to recognize that, over time
and in the long run, the gentry bought oligarchy at a high price and
on terms not all of their own choosing. Had parliamentary oligarchy
been nothing more than a means of establishing the primacy of connection over party, it would have been a simple adjustment of the
court-country relationship in the interests of the conservative rural
gentry; but oligarchy as it emerged was Whig, not Tory, and involved
the growth and dominance of a new politics of public credit,
parliamentary patronage, and an army and navy capable of major action in European and imperial theaters. The connections and
dependencies of county politics became the adjuncts if not the instruments of Walpolean government, and if this role was satisfactory
enough to frustrate all attempts in the tradition of Bolingbroke to
mobilize the country against the court, it could not any longer be supposed that government existed solely to preserve the world of connection and county.

In consequence two things happened. Connections, formed partly
in the county communities and partly in the networks of politics

closer to the centers of power, continued to function as instruments in the process of changing ministries, conducting the rivalries of the oligarchy and cementing the relationship of Crown to Parliament by making the latter the essential area or theater in which the former must find its counselors. Connection became an instrument of national government, not a simple expression of localism; and the appearances of single-party rule were preserved by the circumstance that from 1714 to 1760 it was necessary for every player in the political game to call himself a "Whig" and maintain the quasi-fiction that there persisted a "Tory" threat to the settlements of 1688, 1702, and 1714-16.[6] On the other hand there remained, in the realm of ideology if never fully realized in the realm of behavior, the possibility that a country—or less commonly, a London-based—movement might mobilize national opposition to the normal conduct of oligarchical politics when these went badly. Bolingbroke in 1728-30, Pitt in 1756, Wilkes in the middle 1760's, Wyvill in 1780-84, illustrate this possibility in various ways; but in as many ways the parliamentary system triumphed, and every radical movement—whether Tory or reformist—remained subject to the politics of oligarchy, ministry-formation, and the sovereign need of a stable relationship between Crown and Parliament. Paradoxically, however, the ideology of opposition to the system survived and was exported.

I have reached the third of my paradigm shifts, the one most closely connected with the interpretation of American history. There can be little need to stress that I am referring to what may be termed the Bailyn revolution: the discovery of the extent to which ideologies generated by oppositions within, as well as by opposition to, English parliamentary government in its Walpolean form came to dominate the thinking and to affect the behavior of Americans before, during, and after the Revolution.[7] What may need a little further stressing, I think, is that these ideologies, while English in their sources and provenance, were taken infinitely more seriously in the colonies than in the country of their origin. It was the fact that the English did not act on ideas which they had generated—that they declined to behave as country patriots in revolt against a corrupt government—which persuaded the Revolutionaries that the English people were themselves corrupt. We have to ask ourselves how this remarkable divergence in behavior came to exist. It would be possible to give a Hartzian answer, by suggesting that the ideology in America was a fragment, divorced from its proper context and functioning in uncontrolled and uncontrollable ways.[8] This would in turn lead to debate—a debate which at the moment seems unresolved—aimed at determining how far opposition ideology in America served as a means of expressing real grievances and real perceptions, and how far it was a paranoiac distortion of reality, which drove men mad in the ways so apparent to Governor Hutchinson and his biographer. I imagine it was a good deal of both. We may make an interim approach to the question by saying something about the essential differences between the English context in which opposition thinking was generated and the American context in which it developed.

These essays are in part concerned with questions such as how far the parties and factions of the eighteenth-century colonies may be equated with connections of the familiar kind, and how far with country parties formed to express opposition to patronage and manipulative politics; as well as how far they may have broadened their base, as English country movements before 1714 and after 1760 sometimes did, to include people discontented with their exclusion from the world of oligarchy and even connection. Given that the colonies contained a proportionately larger active electorate than did the United Kingdom, one may well look for tensions of this kind.

The point that seems to need emphasis, however, is that the colonial scene could not duplicate the realities of English politics, inasmuch as a colony was neither a shire nor a nation, and a colonial assembly neither a county meeting nor a parliament. Both before and during the age of oligarchy, a county meeting lacked the formal powers and procedures of an assembly, but the county itself existed in an intimate symbiosis with Parliament which was never possible to the colony. As colonial gentries developed, therefore, they might seek to model themselves on the English political nation, but could never duplicate the conditions under which the latter existed, while finding in their assemblies, both formal and informal, a sounding board unknown in England with which to give voice to their frustrations.

What they could not duplicate was the dual character of the English gentleman and freeman as a being locally influential in his county, but audible and active through his Parliament at court and in town.[9] To bring the grievances of a New England town or a Virginia county to the assembly was never the same thing, since the assembly lacked the authority of Parliament and could not—this I see as entirely crucial—offer the gentleman sources of influence, patronage, and status equal in importance, and intimately related to, those he derived from his neighborhood community. In consequence, the community in America was not to be what it was in England. American politics was not to consist of shires, boroughs, and gentlemen, but of wards, parties, and politicians. On the other hand, however, it might be said that if the colonial gentries were not to develop as a political aristocracy, they were to make a revolution in the attempt to become one. We may consider the crisis of Independence as a profound misunderstanding between the American and English gentries—I am aware that this is only one way of looking at it—as a means of comparing the long-range development of party in the two nations.

An ideal English connection mobilized relationships of influence which arose and were exercised in and through Parliament and the central administration, as well as in and through the shire and its boroughs; and this is true in the seventeenth century, when connections were developed by enlarging the electorate and intensifying the competitiveness of politics, as much as in the eighteenth, when connections were protected by restricting both. It is the symbiosis of shire and Parliament, of country and court, of party and ministry, of the county as expressing the autonomy of the local community and simultaneously giving local effect to the central authority, which must be considered a constant of classical English history and the key to much in English party behavior.

The opposition ideology, developed about 1700 to express discontent with the growing trends toward financial, military, and parliamentary oligarchy, contained, for reasons I need not go into, a good deal which presented executive government as inherently liable to corrupt virtue, that is, to distort the free relationships which ought to exist between government and social personality; and this presentation of government as alien and threatening had an obvious appeal for those, whether within or without the world of the political gentry, who felt themselves excluded from its workings. But because the English social animal felt himself on the contrary directly involved in the government of the Crown—through shire, through Parliament, and through the relationship between the two—an ideology which presented it as alien and as threatening to corrupt him could never express more than half of his mind. With the other half he accepted Parliament and King-in-Parliament, even when governing with an admixture of corruption, as necessary and admirable conditions of his own existence;[10] and when the problem of America reached a climax, in 1774 or in 1783, the English political nation was bound to support the Parliament with which it lived in symbiosis, whether in attempting to coerce the colonies or in consenting to their independence. These were, indeed, but two ways of attaining the same goal: the maintenance of an untrammeled relationship between Parliament and those countries which it could govern. The extent of Parliament's empire was a secondary consideration.

It follows that country parties, which regarded the executive as an alien and hostile force, did not develop—though the idea was formulated—in England while the age of oligarchy lasted; while, that is, the oligarchical or Namierite mode of conducting politics was considered an acceptable mode of conducting the relations between Parliament and nation; whereas in the colonies—which were somewhat less oligarchical and had never been parliamentary societies—there developed a massive and in the end continental country movement which followed the revolutionary path of repudiating parliamentary government itself as corrupt and setting up in its place a republic of separated powers. How far the parties of the pre-Revolutionary colonies displayed country characteristics in embryo I do not know, though I should not be in the least surprised to learn that it was not very much. But the age of oligarchy—a term of art, we should remember, in the historiography of English government—came to an end with revolution in the United States and, about half a century later, with parliamentary reform in the United Kingdom. The rise of a democratic electorate and of democratic mass parties figured in both processes, and we owe it to Richard Hofstadter and William Chambers[11] that we are aware how much earlier the last-named phenomenon appeared in America.

It may be worth concluding with an attempt at generalization concerning the differing roles of democratization under parliamentary and republican conditions.

The American Revolution entailed a rejection of the parliamentary system of government, and of the intimate relationship of executive to legislature expressed in the term "King-in-Parliament." The new nation was to be a republic founded on the separation of powers, but the problems of constructing such a system under continental and federal conditions—in which the failure of gentry to develop as political aristocracy assumed increasing importance—entailed two major consequences. The first of these was a democratic ideology and reality, in which every branch of government appeared as a mode of representation of a highly active electorate.[12] We may call this Madisonian. The second—which we may call Hamiltonian—involved the recognition that the quasi-republican traditions of the English opposition were better at denouncing the role of the executive than at defining it; but when Hamilton seemed to propose reviving the Walpolean mode of government, in which the executive employed patronage to control the legislature, the immediate reaction was visceral. The Revolutionary War had been a civil war only in a submerged sense,[13] and had not polarized parties of opposing principles; the history of Loyalism is the history of Canada; and there is no American equivalent for the way in which Whigs and Tories remembered Parliamentarians and Royalists. But because the ideological foundations of the Revolution lie in a deep schism within Whig values, the Federalists and Republicans of the 1790's seemed to one another to offer differing interpretations of what the Revolution had been—the former scenting subversion and the latter betrayal[14]—and until 1800 there persisted, as there had in England until 1714, the danger of a breakdown of legitimacy.

But Hofstadter, Chambers, and others[15] show us how the growth of organized mass participation encouraged legitimation by converting, and dissolving, opposed political principles into issues capable of

widespread appeal to a fairly integrated electorate. Democratization
was an instrument of mobilization, of symbiosis between the nation
and its government, just as the English county community had
served to integrate the country with the court. The ward—an inven-
tion of Jefferson's, we are told—served in the room of the county; an
instrument of democracy and at the same time of corruption. For
patronage developed along with participation; Hamilton too was a
prophet of popular politics; and with the failure of American
aristocracy, new democrat was but old Whig writ large.[16]

In Britain during the next century, the heirs of the ruling Whigs
turned cautiously in the direction, not certainly of democracy, but of
enlargement and reorganization of the electorate. The growth of
oligarchy was being reversed at last, as it was found that the stability
of government required a wider machinery of consultation and participation, on a scale which the traditional counties and boroughs
were ceasing to satisfy. Yet the essentials of parliamentary government survived the death of the shire which had been its foundation.
Electorates and party organizations—in which the dispensation of
patronage shrank in importance as in America it increased—served as
means of providing parliamentary majorities, which in turn were
means of determining the composition of ministries; the function of
Parliament continued to be that of furnishing the executive with
counselors answerable to itself. Party in both Britain and America
was a means of connecting the electorate to its government; but there
remains the antithesis that parliamentary democracy is medieval, an
extension and transcendence of the idea of the community of the
realm, whereas republican democracy is classical, an extension and
transcendence of the idea of the balance of the component parts. The
British observer beholds with starting eyes the debate in which the
Presidential candidates of 1976 seriously discussed whether the
President should or should not be of the same party as the majority in
Congress. What role the parties and factions of the eighteenth-
century colonies played in this great divergence of political
understanding is for others to determine.

Religion and Politics in Revolutionary New England: Natural Rights Reconsidered

Stephen Botein

In 1773, toward the end of an oration commemorating the "Bloody Tragedy" of the Boston Massacre, Benjamin Church was moved to summarize almost a century of politics in New England. "PARTIES and factions since the days of the detested *Andross*," he proclaimed, "have been strangers to this land; no distinctions of heart-felt animosity disturbed the peace and order of society . . . ."[1] However dubious as history, this brief retrospective was revealing of the ideological framework within which many New Englanders perceived and interpreted political conflict. In theory, if not in practice, organized competition for power was considered abnormal, requiring explanation in terms of extreme or "heart-felt" divisions within the community. Although the everyday realities of politics in eighteenth-century New England often deviated from consensual norms, it was the habit of ideologues in the region to characterize political struggles as exceptional events.[2]

One corollary of this approach to politics was that New Englanders tended to justify divisive political action arising from disputes over specific measures or policies by reference to the most fundamental of principles, designating some political behavior lawful precisely and only because other behavior could be pronounced unlawful. They were "very notional" in their politics, as one Revolutionary polemicist observed of Bostonians in particular, and this mentality was registered in political language that stressed not considerations of utility or interest but constitutional rights and obligations.[3] By examining such language closely during the greatest political struggle

13

of the century, the controversy over British imperial policy that culminated in Independence, it may be possible to understand better the
social as well as the intellectual sources of pre-modern attitudes
toward party and faction underlying public discourse in late colonial
New England.

The legal arguments with which New Englanders tried to justify
their political opposition to English imperial rule in the decade following passage of the Stamp Act have not gone unnoticed in the history
of the American Revolution, but recent scholarship has been unap-
preciative of their importance. This failure of attention has both
reflected and contributed to a broader pattern of historiographical
neglect. Although it has been a commonplace ever since Burke's
"Speech on Conciliation" that lawyers were prominent in the leadership of the Patriot movement, the place of legal conceptions in
Revolutionary ideology has seldom engaged historians. It is a
neglected topic in the history of a period so intensively studied that
few of its political byways, however obscure, have not been thoroughly explored.[4]

One explanation of this apparently large scholarly lacuna is that
from a technical perspective legal thought was of only limited significance in the literature of the Revolutionary movement. While elo-
quently declaiming the blessings of the common law, Patriot ideologues—whether trained in the law or not—were apt to cite judicial
decisions or legislation casually and with vague intent, showing far
less sense of specificity than the English jurists they professed most
to admire. Or they became hopelessly entangled in dubious readings
of a few arcane dicta, notably Coke's. Very possibly, this was for a
good reason. By the orthodox standards of mid-eighteenth-century
English political theory, the Patriots appear to have had a bad case,
at odds especially with prevailing views of parliamentary power. Ac-
cordingly, recent "ideological" interpreters of the Revolution have
been disinclined to emphasize the specifically legal content of the
great debates conducted in the 1760's and 1770's. Law, they assume,
was peripheral to the absorbing diagnostic interest of the Revolutionary generation in malignant power and corruption; it was not a key
element of the "transforming" ideology that shaped perceptions

and action in the decade before Independence.[5]

Nearly half a century has passed since law in one sense or another figured prominently in the historical literature devoted to the Revolution. What attracted the interest of scholars then was not positive but *natural* law, as a source of *natural* rights. Once upon a time, it may be recalled, John Locke was thought to have been the Father of the Revolution, and natural rights theory seemed to reflect its creative egalitarian potential.[6] It was a theory, too, that some historians observed had been most favored by New Englanders; this was so even if Jefferson and other enlightened polemicists to the south, modishly in touch with French political thought, came to be better known for their habit of reference to "certain unalienable rights." As a source of constitutional discussion, Boston was very much "the Metropolis of Sedition" that the Loyalist Peter Oliver later recalled.[7]

To be sure, the natural rights theory that figured prominently in the legal argumentation of Revolutionary New Englanders did not draw solely or even primarily on lawyers' language, which may be why it has often been treated not as legal thought at all but simply as rhetorical strategy of last resort—the disruptive implications or effects of which may or may not have been clear or agreeable to those who originally articulated it.[8] Indeed, as students of eighteenth-century Puritanism have always known, natural rights argumentation has been an important component of the political doctrines regularly preached by New England clergymen well before the first exchanges of imperial controversy in the 1760's. And Congregational ministers, Oliver's "black Regiment," were among its most insistent and copious proponents in the Revolutionary crisis.[9] It was, furthermore, a mode of constitutional discussion—a vocabulary—that pervaded the sermons of clergymen affiliated with most of the major religious factions in eighteenth-century New England. Hence, perhaps, the almost perverse inattention to such discourse in recent studies of Revolutionary American religion. Since these studies have tended to make a point of associating the Revolutionary impulse with "anti-legalists" in the traditionalist camp of New England's fragmented religious scene, natural law and natural rights have seemed both too ecumenical and too formalistic for the stuff of a truly

Revolutionary religious vocabulary.[10]

In what follows it should be apparent that from the outset of the Revolutionary crisis references to what was repeatedly said to be the "Law of Nature" and "those Rights of Mankind which flow from it" filled the writings of many Patriot ideologues in New England—clergymen especially but lawyers and other pamphleteers as well. Natural rights theory should once again be taken seriously, as a mode of legal argument operative in the public forum of Revolutionary New England. As a way to label political behavior lawful or unlawful, it was acknowledged and cited by both sides in the controversy, and therefore in one sense cannot be said to have been "determinative": it did not always compel Patriot conclusions and exclude others.[11] At a functional minimum, however, natural rights theory was the source of a recognizable and possibly essential vocabulary that allowed New Englanders to legitimize active political opposition, outside the legislative arena as well as within, to English imperial policies.[12]

It was, furthermore, a vocabulary grounded in the personal and social experience of those who used it. For many New Englanders, it seemed more applicable than common law to the large public issues of the 1760's and 1770's because it shaped those issues into patterns that had special meanings in the context of earlier thought and practice. For some Patriots in the region, it was a vocabulary reflective of experience that may actually have structured their basic awareness of reality during the imperial crisis.[13] This, it may be speculated, was the edge of its appeal, despite sentence after sentence of seemingly vaporous abstraction.

While some Patriot proponents of natural rights theory quoted and may even have studied such Continental jurists as Pufendorf, Burlamaqui, and Vattel, the sources New Englanders found most congenial—"purer fountains," according to James Otis—were English. Milton was mentioned ritually, and other prominent English devotees of natural rights who may be said to have been influential included

Sidney, Harrington, Lord Somers, and Hoadly.[14] Cited most frequently and confidently, however, was "the great Mr. LOCK," whose
political treatises were probably revered as much by those who had
never consulted them as by those who had.[15] For the most part, New
Englanders drew on political writings in tune with the principles of
the Glorious Revolution, and with the stabilizing spirit of rationality
that had permeated English political discourse by the end of the
seventeenth century—in contrast with the volatile appeals to
"reason" of an earlier age.[16]

In Revolutionary New England, as previously in England, natural
rights argumentation was likely to follow certain patterns and thus
may be credited with a methodology of its own. A general outline of
this methodology may be derived from a reading of polemical
literature published in the region during the Revolutionary years.[17]

A natural rights argument was, first of all, a normative statement
based on the "nature and reason of things," or—to use a word with
legal connotations—their very "constitution." Eager to establish the
impossibility of contrary thought, natural rights proponents insisted
that their reasonings were "conformable to axioms of immutable
truth." These were the "principles of nature and eternal reason" that
so moved John Adams; these were principles so inescapable that efforts at mere "logical proof" could be compared—in John Hancock's
words—to "burning tapers at noon-day, to assist the sun in enlightening the world . . . ."[18] Natural rights were said to represent the
shared understanding of humankind, or the "nature of man"; from
their "very obvious" truths no reasonable human being could or
would dissent. As the most self-evident of such truths, the law of self-
preservation, or self-defense, reflected a moral necessity "fixed and
immutable, from the beginning to the end of time." Here was the
"great and universal law of nature," so irresistible that it was built into man's biological structure; here was the basic right that God had
breathed into humanity, opposition to which—as Scripture
taught—was "murder."[19]

More particularly, what gave a natural rights argument the appearance of completeness was a demonstration that it was "agreeable
to the common sense and experience of mankind," as located in the

"history of all nations and ages."[20] With what has been termed the historical "permissiveness" habitual to the era, natural rights proponents assumed that the essential purposes and needs of all communities, past and present, were uniform and readily recoverable—as if all epochs were equidistant from the contemporary observer. History thus furnished constitutional "precedents" to natural rights proponents, who could apply to such material the standard "analogical" techniques of reasoning that were typical of their day. Here the methodology of natural rights argumentation overlapped with that of political writers more concerned to describe the behavioral uniformities of statecraft than to proclaim its moral requirements. In arguing natural rights, the critical question was not so much whether a proposition accorded with what had always happened as whether it reproduced what had always been thought.[21] If properly "founded in nature," a natural right would of necessity have been "fully display'd" under "different forms" and "different meridians." It would be "so plain a dictate of reason and observation" as to have been sustained by the "general concurrent testimony of the wisest and best in all ages."[22]

Since natural rights were "confirmed . . . by the revealed Will of God," recorded in the Charter of Revelation as well as in Nature, Scripture was an important source of relevant examples. After all, "rules of right conduct" derived not only from the "reason of things" and the "nature of man" but "above all the will of God, the supreme Lawgiver." Hence the "inspired writers" were "not wanting in the best admonitions about our temporals."[23] Precisely to what extent Scripture and natural law did or had to coincide was not always certain, especially as the model of theocracy contained in the Old Testament troubled many New Englanders. If natural law was based on the "unchangeable nature of the Deity," being a "transcript of his moral perfections," it might follow that even its "smallest iota" could not be disregarded or abrogated. On the other hand, it might be argued, a revelation "pretending to be of GOD" that contradicted any part of natural law—presumably as it was registered in the "nature of things"—was "immediately to be rejected as imposture; for the Deity cannot make a law contrary to the law of nature, without acting contrary to himself." Furthermore, this or that Scriptural episode might appropriately be interpreted as an "extraordinary vouchsafement" or "signal favor" of God to the Jewish people. In any case, although some specific natural rights were sustained by the "express appointment of God," others inhered in situations where no such "special directions" were obtainable.[24]

Clergymen would normally begin their disquisitions by focusing on a Biblical text, but afterward—if Israel were "deem'd an exception to the rest of mankind," as one of their number cheerfully explained—they might proceed to survey pagan antiquity. The "common sentiments of antiquity" preserved in the recorded words of such luminaries as Plato, Aristotle, and Cicero were powerfully supportive of a natural rights argument. Flagrantly "shocking iniquity" was surely unthinkable not only to "good christians" but also to "good citizens and patriots of Greece and Rome."[25]

Also enlightening was the record of modern European thought, notably that of England—which was presumed to embody better than any other nation's the common sense of humanity. The wisdom of the English past was distilled in its constitution. Natural rights might be "inalienable," granted by no one except perhaps God, but Magna Charta and lesser constitutional law could be considered "declaratory" or "in affirmance" of them. One reason that *Calvin's Case* was so favored by Patriot writers was that Coke there had more to say about natural law than in his other cases altogether. This accorded with the sense of New Englanders that much of the English common law was suffused with the higher morality of nature. It was providential, indeed, that God had placed New England under the English constitution, a scheme of things "founded in the law of God and of nature;—on the principles of reason and equity."[26]

Just what specific rights were natural to mankind, apart from the right to life defined by the law of self-preservation, was of course more problematic than the methodology by which those rights were to be articulated. One natural right, undoubtedly, was the right of every man "to dispose of his *own* property," a proposition to which clergymen were as firmly committed as the laity. "Property is prior to all human laws, institutions and charters," it was asserted in one ser-

mon. *"God hath given the earth to the children of men."* For if rulers
"can take away one penny from us against our wills," argued one Son
of Liberty, "they can take all. If they have such power over our prop-
erties they must have a proportionable power over our persons; and
from hence it will follow, that they can demand and take away our
lives . . . ." This would be a condition contradicting the most fundamental natural law.[27]

Another natural right of paramount significance to most New
Englanders was the right of everyone "to examine and judge for
himself, in matters of religion; and to worship God according to the
dictates of conscience . . . ." Confirmed by the gospel injunction
that individuals "search the scriptures," the natural right of conscience could be regarded as "sacred" too. If some traditionalist
clergymen occasionally chose to make a sharp distinction between the
"birth-right" of men in a "worldly or natural kingdom" and the rights
they enjoyed "by grant of CHRIST," most avoided the issue by claim-
ing or simply assuming that civil and religious privileges were "nearly related, each one being a part of the grand whole . . . ." Thus New
Englanders might possess their liberties "not merely as men,
originally created in GOD's image, holding a distinguished rank in his
creation, but also as Christians, redeemed by the blood of CHRIST."[28]

From another perspective, the rights of nature could be understood
so expansively as to defy enumeration. Whether some were less
"fundamental" and therefore could be "surrendered" in certain circumstances was often unclear. Opinions varied from one writer to
another and even within the same sermon or political tract. But it was
generally agreed that when men formed into civil societies they gave
up at most only a fraction of their total natural freedom—that "pre-
cious commodity" of which all were "equally original proprietors"
and to "every branch" of which they might retain at least some
rights. "The great and wise Author of our being," observed one
clergyman, "has so formed us, that the love of liberty is natural."
Depending on the exigencies of a particular time and place, men
might therefore assert a wide variety of natural rights, not only to life
and property and conscience but also—for example—to "the best im-
provement of all their powers, with every reasonable and equitable

advantage they have to promote their present and everlasting welfare." In short, "happiness," or those "natural privileges" essential to its achievement, might well be enclosed within the protective language of natural law; to some New Englanders, clergymen included, this was a multifaceted fundamental right that could not be resigned in any social order, despite the "mutual consent" of those in whom it had been vested.[29]

Ultimately, the crucial legal issue faced by proponents of natural rights in Revolutionary New England was contractual. The problem, identified pointedly in one sermon, was to know "where power ends and liberty begins," and here—for all their vagueness and inconsistency—natural rights proponents could be suggestively eloquent on behalf of liberty. "Dominion, or right to rule," according to one formulation, "is evidently founded neither in nature or grace, but compact, and consideration: antecedent whereto, one has no better right to rule than another."[30] What, then, if a ruler were to adopt measures that threatened the natural rights of his subjects? Answers to this question differed in their particulars. Some indicated that such behavior would have to be contrary to either the explicit or the implicit terms—or both—of the compact from which the government originated, thus constituting a "forfeiture" or "default" that dissolved the reciprocal obligation of the people to obey their magistrates. "CONTRACTS," one clergyman proclaimed, "are sacred things"; faithful performance, it could be maintained, was itself a requirement of natural law. Others, sometimes without the most complex of theoretical understanding, seemed to argue more starkly that a political compact was "void" or "illegal," whatever its terms once a ruler invaded such undeniably fundamental rights of nature as life, property, and conscience.[31] Whatever the precise formulation, it was the final function of natural rights argumentation to determine the critical moment when resistance to tyranny was justified.

"In all disputes between power and liberty," it had been said in late Stuart England, "power must always be proved, but liberty proves itself; the one being founded on positive law, the other upon the law of nature." Natural rights, revealed in numerous instances of "the people's setting up, and pulling down their monarchs for their tyranny," were solid enough to sustain the lawfulness of extraordinary political behavior.[32] For New Englanders, convinced as most were that the British constitution was largely "excellent" in theory, events following 1765 forced them to distinguish the "natural" elements of their positive law from "unnatural" practices. Because "certain essential rights" of Englishmen were "founded in the law of God and nature" and thus were the "common rights of mankind," argued Samuel Adams at the very beginning of the imperial crisis, New Englanders were "unalienably entitled" to them regardless of any "law of society."[33]

Whether such a case could be maintained successfully in any conventional legal forum was open to question,[34] but this was not the only or even the principal purpose of such argumentation. In the midst of a transatlantic political struggle, Patriot ideologues in New England needed a legal vocabulary of sufficient gravity to warrant deviation from the consensual norms of eighteenth-century politics, and natural rights theory was conveniently applicable to situations in which the most vital of political concerns were said to be involved. How and why people might agree to associate and dissociate were the large if elusive problems that New Englanders approached by citing natural rights. Potentially they were indeed the "revolution principles" with which John Adams, writing as "Novanglus" early in 1775, sought to summon up opposition to the mother country.[35]

It must be asked why arguments derived from theory that was largely out of fashion in England[36] should have been persuasive to many New Englanders. In the great struggle of the late seventeenth century against the Dominion of New England, references to natural law had not been abundant; most frequently, as their Revolutionary descendants were aware, opponents of Governor Andros had chosen to rest their case against tyranny upon their "title to the common rights of *Englishmen*."[37] Less than a century later, New Englanders were more inclined and better prepared to argue their natural rights over and against the stipulations of English positive law. The significance of their increasing reliance on such a fundamental legal vocabulary must be understood in broad historical context.

As frontal conflict with the mother country intensified, it may be that the uneasy relationship in the minds of New Englanders between natural and common law came to resonate against basic incongruities of political experience in the colonies, where realities of power and social structure diverged markedly from the formal arrangements of empire. If some New Englanders, whether Patriot or Tory, were eager to show that they considered themselves "subjects of common LAW,"[38] possibly sensing that this was an emblem of status for provincial gentry, many others were willing to support their cause on the basis of insights into the "nature of things" arising out of peculiarly American practices and assumptions. It may be, too, that the still rudimentary condition of the legal community in eighteenth-century New England helps to explain why one important legal vocabulary of the Revolutionary movement was not distinctively a lawyer's vocabulary at all. Lacking the intricate intellectual and institutional apparatus of a more developed legal system, the colonists of New England—most of whom were said to know a little law, few of whom appeared to know much—may have been especially well disposed to accept as law an argument advanced so frequently by clergymen. That this was a legal argument grounded in the Book of Nature, too, was not altogether surprising in a society where law books were scarce, and Nature abundant.[39]

Some historians have assumed that eighteenth-century New Englanders were inclined to propound natural rights because of traditional Puritan preoccupation with divine law,[40] yet the religious origins of such Revolutionary argumentation were more immediate and specific. The broad appeal of natural rights theory in New England is perhaps best understood in the context of ecclesiastical experience during the half century preceding Independence. Before the Revolutionary crisis began, the clergymen of the region—and, it is fair to suggest, many members of their congregations—had become practiced in a mode of legal argument that stressed contractual rights grounded in Nature, or Nature's God, because as clergymen or members of congregations they had frequently been obliged to confront fundamental ecclesiastical issues that could be and were discussed in those terms. New Englanders may be said to have thereby developed and deepened the habit of arguing on the basis of natural rights, or in analagous patterns on the basis of "Christian" rights.

One problem of perennial concern in eighteenth-century New England was the nature of the relationship between a minister and his congregation. That this was in some sense a contractual relationship, in fact as well as theory, was certain; that the terms of the contract were often in dispute, because of economics as much as theology, was inescapable. Outside of Boston, Cotton Mather had observed in 1700, ministers "do make their *Contracts* with their people, to their *Stipends.*" Repeatedly in the decades that followed, despite a commitment by the secular authorities to enforce those contracts, severe inflation—aggravated by sectarian conflict, particularly bitter during and after the Great Awakening—caused ministers and their congregations to quarrel over their respective rights and obligations.[41]

Even at the most mundane level of negotiation, ministers were apt to emphasize natural or related Christian rights. If they complained that the real value of their salaries had declined, they knew their congregations would accuse them of being "wholly *Govern'd by self-interest.*" Yet surely ministers themselves could not be expected to resign what was lawfully theirs. If their affairs became urgent, they could exercise the "Christian liberty"—acknowledged by many to be natural as well—of packing up and leaving. "The law of self-preservation is binding," noted one outraged clergyman by way of explaining his decision to abandon the sacred profession altogether.[42]

A more elevated argument, often enhanced by word play, would reason from an analogy between the relationship of a clergyman to his congregation and that of a ruler to his people. From one point of view, the doctrine that rulers were "God's ministers" could generate "compliment and adulation" of civil government, as Jonathan Mayhew remarked with disapproval in his Massachusetts Election Sermon of 1754. But other conclusions were possible, and furthermore—as Mayhew put it—"very applicable, not only to civil Rulers, but also to those whom our blessed Lord has *counted faithful, putting them into the ministry.'"⁴³*

A clergyman of traditionalist leanings might call the contract a "covenant," and refer to "Christian liberties" instead of natural rights, but the logic of the relationship defined by such language—including legitimate reasons for termination—could be governed by principles similar to those commonly said to constitute natural law in the secular realm. Injury to or failure of performance by one of the parties was what mattered. So, in 1747, a young minister named John Cleaveland drew up a "Plain Narrative" to defend a group that had recently withdrawn from the Second Church in Ipswich and chosen him as their new spiritual leader. Postulating that a covenant bound minister and people, Cleaveland contended that by failing to preach doctrines of grace or to promote the operations of the Holy Spirit the Second Church's pastor had neglected to fulfill the duties "presupposed" of him by those who had joined the church. Thus the covenant was dissolved, and all claims he might try to make to the obedience of his people were invalid. Since the pastor and his allies within the church had acted as "Aggressors," the "extra-judicial" behavior of those who had withdrawn was "lawful," or at least "excusable."⁴⁴

A Harvard-educated Arminian clergyman, on the other hand, was likely to be sympathetic to clerical prerogative, even if more receptive than his orthodox colleagues to the libertarian language of London dissent. Ministers like Mayhew, Charles Chauncy, and Ebenezer Gay, also thinking in contractual terms, were concerned to limit the right of a congregation to depose its pastor. "They who are employ'd in the Work of the Ministry, are to exercise a *spiritual Government in the Church of GOD,"* observed Gay in 1742. "They are constituted Rulers over GOD's Household, and Obedience to them is plainly required." Nevertheless, reflecting a sense of the question that transcended the religious divisions of the region, Gay knew that the authority of ministers was not indefinite. As he told the Massachusetts Convention of Ministers in 1746, "spiritual Pastors are not to exercise the *Lordship,* which secular Princes are wont to do, in ruling with a high Hand, and according to their own Will and Pleasure." If a pastor abused his authority, his friend Chauncy had told the same assemblage previously, he "forfeited all Right to the good Opinion of Men . . ."[45]

What then? The Arminians of the Boston area were not necessarily at odds here with Calvinists like John Cleaveland, although of course there were few clergymen at all who cared to articulate and examine critically the theoretical niceties of the issue. "[Stand] up in defence of your christian liberty," Mayhew advised, against those who "shall attempt to exercise any kinds of spiritual tyranny over you." According to Gay, no one was "more worthy to be rejected of GOD, and all the People," than a bad minister. If these were vague words, suggesting no specific remedy, during the Revolutionary crisis Gay was prepared to be somewhat more precise. In 1768, though no partisan himself of the American cause, he undertook to define the pastoral role by borrowing directly from the same vocabulary that others were applying to the transatlantic political situation. "The end of a minister's coming unto a people," he explained, "sheweth that it should be at their desire, or by their consent." This proposition Gay supported in two ways. First, "the gospel confirms this to them, in the liberty it gives them of choosing, or consenting to, their own pastor, to whom they commit the care of their souls." Furthermore, by the "law of self-preservation," people have a "natural right to provide for the safety of their souls . . ." To deny this right—or "Christian liberty"—would be spiritual tyranny, to which submission was not required.[46]

The issue of pastoral authority did not usually stand alone, in any case, but was enclosed in more general considerations of the rights of conscience against the authority of the civil and ecclesiastical powers. Discussing the larger problem, which became acute following the schismatic turmoil of the Great Awakening, both Arminians and their Calvinist brethren often had recourse to natural rights theory. Except among Connecticut's outspoken supporters of religious uniformity, it was becoming increasingly apparent to New Englanders—"from the Make of Human Nature, itself," as their dissenting friends in London liked to say—that mankind would persist in differing on points of religion. Gaining ground throughout the region at mid-century was what President Clap of Yale caustically termed a "New Scheme of Religion," by which it was maintained that "every Man" had a "Right to judge *for himself.*"[47] Among the authors of the "Scheme" Clap had in mind were the Arminian clergy of the Boston area, who indeed believed—in Charles Chauncy's words—that coercion in "Matters of Religion and Conscience" was "not only contrary to the *Example of Christ,* and the *Precepts of his Gospel;* but to the *Nature and Reason of Things.*" Rulers who failed to follow this maxim neglected their duty "to make Men happy in the Enjoyment of their Rights, whether *natural* or *Christian.*" But such inspiring sentiments were not peculiar to Arminians. In 1744, for example, Connecticut's Elisha Williams—a lawyer as well as a clergyman—demonstrated that a true friend of the revival could make as eloquent use of Locke as a Bostonian could. Pleading for the "essential Rights and Liberties of Protestants" against repressive colonial legislation, Williams was emphatic in pronouncing *"this Right of private Judgment,* and *worshipping* GOD according to their *Consciences"* to be the *"natural and unalienable Right of every Men,* what Men by entering into civil Society neither did, nor could give up into the Hands of the Community . . . ." Despite a different theological background, his views thus converged with those of Boston's adventurers in "proto-Unitarian" heresy.[48]

In other situations, for different reasons, clergymen in New England asserted the rights of private judgment or conscience for themselves and members of their congregations within a common historical understanding that conferred special significance on their region. Revivalists fighting anti-itinerancy laws in Connecticut and Boston clergymen warning against Archbishop Secker's design to "Espicopize" the colonies could agree that they were the descendants of men and women who had left England in pursuit of an opportunity to enjoy their rights—Christian or natural—to religious freedom. This was the *"grand motive"* of the colonists' migration, as Chauncy summed up the eighteenth-century version of the Puritan past, and his fellow ministers expounded the theme tirelessly on a variety of ceremonial occasions.[49] Having so removed themselves from England for reasons of conscience, New Englanders could not lawfully be forced to resubmit to religious dictation, whether by hard-line Congregationalists in Connecticut or by ambitious Anglicans said to be plotting the overthrow of the New England Way. At stake, in either case, was the right to "withdraw" from "usurped power"—as Ebenezer Gay had once phrased it. To a New Light clergyman it might better be called a justifiable exercise of "Christian liberty," while in the eyes of the Connecticut authorities it amounted to "rebellion against the state." From their divergent perspectives, both revivalists and Arminians could still share the relevant historical "precedents"—the withdrawal of Protestants from Rome and that of Puritans from the English Church. Further in the background was the departure of Israel from Egypt.[50]

Regularly engaged in immediate debate of such matters for decades before passage of the Stamp Act, clergymen in New England continued to articulate natural rights theory long after its heyday had passed in the mother country. Hence, from the beginning of the Revolutionary controversy, they were intellectually equipped and perhaps predisposed to use a legal vocabulary that would shape a case for opposition and later resistance on the basis of the laws of Nature and Nature's God. With the help of other New Englanders—lawyers included, some of whom had participated as laymen in previous ecclesiastical conflicts—clergymen were thus able and ready to confer legitimacy on political behavior of which the lawfulness, by the consensual norms of New England's early political life, might otherwise have been in doubt.

Fundamentals of natural rights theory figured variously in the specific Revolutionary argumentation of New Englanders. Once matters had come to a head, it might suffice simply to cite the law of self-preservation to justify resistance to coercive imperial policy. Earlier, the natural right to dispose of one's own property was obviously at stake amid a controversy over parliamentary tax measures, and the natural right to follow one's own conscience could form the basis of further opposition to a government that was perhaps in collusion with designing Anglicans to deprive New England of its religious liberties.[51] But the decisive natural rights argument of the Revolution was that which defined the limits of obedience to unjust rulers in contractual terms. This argument took aim at the king, and was thoroughly articulated in New England well before Tom Paine—attacking George III in *Common Sense*—asserted flatly, without elaboration, that Independence was a necessity, anything else being "repugnant to reason, the universal order of things, to all examples from former ages."[52] The most strenuous proponents of natural rights, as argued against the Crown, were the clergymen of New England.

And, in the spring and summer of 1775, John Cleaveland—using words similar to those with which he had justified failure to obey pastoral commands in Ipswich some three decades earlier—announced in the Essex *Gazette,* under the pen name of "Johannes in Eremo," that King George had committed a "breach of covenant" and thus dissolved the colonists' obligation of allegiance. Whether or not the mind of this small town Calvinist was "narrow, dark and groveling," as the Arminian Mayhew had once charged, it is apparent that Cleaveland's vocabulary was related to that which Mayhew himself had used as far back as 1750, when his celebrated "Discourse Concerning Unlimited Submission" proclaimed the "natural and legal rights of the people, against the unnatural and illegal encroachments of arbitrary power."[53]

Well before Cleaveland presented his case against the king, some of his bretheren in New England had indicated unmistakably that revolutionary change was a likely outcome of the crisis. George's right to rule might "cease," observed one Baptist preacher in 1773. If evil ministers of the king continued to act as "rebels to GOD, and the laws and rights of nature," then it might be permissible for the colonists to resume the power that was always ultimately theirs, even while the king held it as their trustee. Somewhat more cautiously, as befits an Arminian, Gad Hitchcock took the occasion of the Massachusetts Election Sermon in 1774 to warn that rulers, being trustees of the people, should be "well acquainted with human nature and the natural rights of mankind," lest the people determine rightfully to "resume" the authority they had granted and "transfer" it to others.[54]

This, however, was merely the conclusion of a more extensive argument from natural rights that had begun to emerge almost from the beginning of the imperial controversy. It was an argument that echoed the long Protestant saga of removal or separation from tyranny preached ritually by the clergymen of New England in response to the dangers, real or anticipated, of Anglican and sometimes local Congregational Establishment. Without neglecting the legal rights supposedly guaranteed to all English by Magna Charta, English statutes, and English courts, some New Englanders—often though by no means always clergymen—argued along lines with larger metaphorical implications. The relevant historical setting, in their minds, was a drama of political withdrawal and reassociation. Increasingly, another withdrawal seemed necessary.

The argument that took form in the Revolutionary literature of New England was simple in its outlines, with room for variation in detail. The original settlers of the region, motivated by their "sacred thirst" for religious liberty, decided to "bid a final *adieu* to all the delights of their native country" and "quietly withdrew themselves" to the New World. They had occupied the American wilderness on their own, not as agents of the English government, whereupon all rights of the mother country to govern them without their direct consent lapsed. Having left the realm, according to one formalistic version of this mythic history, the colonists had established "distinct states"—a proposition so stark that Edward Bancroft, representing the colonists' cause in England, wondered whether it was "agreeable to their Wishes."[55]

For some New Englanders it definitely was, and they went on to draw sweeping conclusions. In so doing, they adapted an argument that Jeremiah Dummer had presented long before, with a somewhat different understanding of historical sequence, in his celebrated *Defence of the New-England Charters*. Having withdrawn from the realm, it was claimed, the colonists had entered into a limited contractual relationship not with Parliament but with the Crown alone, guaranteeing certain traditional English rights—specified in charters—that were granted on the condition or for the consideration that the colonists improve their territories, presumably for the diplomatic and commercial benefit of the mother country. "What we enjoy by charter," so one New Englander affirmed in 1769, "is not to be looked upon barely as matter of grace . . . . Our fathers faithfully performed the conditions, on which charter privileges were granted." While being "productive of great advantage to the mother country," they had personally been obliged to exchange the comforts of their "pleasant seats and fertile fields" in England for the "innumerable perils" of "these then barbarous shores"; as even some Englishmen were willing to acknowledge, they had endured "Hardships almost beyond the Power of Language to describe." Who could calculate the "SUM" with which they had purchased their privileges, venturing "not only their estates but their persons" in the task of subduing a "wild, uncultivated wilderness, inhabited by savage beasts, and more savage men"? The first New Englanders had thus "widely extended the *British* dominions, at their *own* expence, without any charge to the mother country from which they came." Surely that had been sufficiently "valuable" consideration, according to the terms of Dummer's formulation, in return for charter rights that in any case were said by some merely to affirm rights enshrined in natural law.[56]

The king, then, had no right of sovereignty over the colonists by virtue of his crown as King of Great Britain, only a right to govern on the basis of the particular stipulations of agreement contained in different colonial charters. The terms of these agreements with England were themselves protected—as contractual rights—by principles of natural law, and thus could not lawfully be altered by means of subsequent legislation or judicial decisions. To try to alter them would be a "shameful Breach of public Faith" unworthy of *"Turks"* and *"Pagans,"* not to mention *"Christianized Britons,"* since "Reason, Right, and Equity" cried out so strongly against such treatment of those who with their blood had mastered the land. Whether correctly or not from a narrow legalistic point of view, Charles Chauncy noted, his countrymen "really thought" their rights and privileges were "unalienable upon the foot of justice by any power on earth." New Englanders were "universally informed of their CHARTER RIGHTS," according to Benjamin Church in his Massacre Oration of 1773. They amounted to a *"patrimony,"* it was said, purchased *"dearly"* by the

first settlers and regarded by later generations as their "richest in-
heritance." It was a compelling duty of the descendants to protect
this legacy. "Were our noble ancestors, who came over to this country
for the sake of liberty," proclaimed one clergyman in 1776, "to rise
from their graves, and make their appearance on the stage, at this
day; with what inflamed indignation would they behold that system
of oppression and slavery which has been lately formed against New
England and America . . . ."[57]

John Cleaveland summed it all up, from a Calvinist perspective of
1771, in two issues of the Essex *Gazette*. The Puritan removal to
America had marked the end of all necessary subjection to the Crown,
he explained, as the founders of New England had exercised
their"natural Right of Migration" for the sake of conscience. Having
purchased land "with their own Money" from "Indian Princes," they
had full authority to establish an "independent State or Government
of their own." Instead, they had compacted with the mother country
for aid and protection; but should England exceed its authority and
make an "Infraction" of the compact, or covenant, the colonists
would be relieved of their obligations and could then rightfully
withdraw once again from tyranny. In Cleaveland's mind, it seems,
separation was both a historical fact and a fundamental option
underlying American claims. Hence the special meaning of his in-
troductory rhetorical flourish four years later—"GREAT-BRITAIN
adieu!"—as he began his presentation of the case against the king.[58]

Here, evidently, was the core of a legal vocabulary that proved of
consequence in the rush of events toward Independence. That it was a
vocabulary of sufficient power to legitimize political activity in opposition to the policies of the mother country may be explained, in
part, by the way it reflected eighteenth-century Protestant versions
of world history as a drama of repeated withdrawals. If clergymen in
New England were well prepared and inclined to preach such doctrines on account of their grinding experience with ecclesiastical conflict over half a century, doubtless many laymen—sometimes
veterans themselves of such conflict—were especially responsive too.
The broad contours of the story were familiar. Within New England,
natural rights theory provided perhaps the most broadly popular con-

stitutional vocabulary of the Revolutionary movement. In that context it may have been particularly significant that one New England clergyman, in 1777, could speak of the "separation that hath taken place, between the United States of America and Great-Britain," or that another could interpret the behavior of the principals in that broken relationship as "acting over" the parts of Pharaoh and Israel.[59] Metaphorically, at some level of regional consciousness, the Revolution could be viewed as yet another large folk decision to separate from tyranny.

Having reached a climax in the first paragraphs of the Declaration of Independence, natural rights theory began to disappear from the public discourse of Americans, New Englanders included. By the mid-1780's it was apparent that architects of the new republican order preferred to rely on written constitutional provisions instead of basic moral law to determine the boundaries between liberty and power. For clergymen who had so vigorously promoted natural rights during the crisis, it was a predictable development. Having been delivered from bondage under the leadership of a Moses, as Washington was to be known, they may have understood that sooner or later fundamentals would have to be codified.[60]

That this happened sooner rather than later is possibly explained by the larger incongruity of natural rights in the emerging politics of post-Revolutionary America. The argumentative methodology of moral constitutionalism was incompatible not only with the need perceived by some to stabilize a new society but with widespread democratic aspirations based on theories of popular sovereignty. Presupposing as it did a normative consensus within the body politic, which was presumed to be more or less passive except in moments of extraordinary crisis, natural rights theory rested on assumptions of legitimacy that excluded the possibility of continuing political competition by diverse interest groups. It was at once too radical and too conservative.[61]

In New England, the waning relevance of this constitutional

vocabulary was nicely registered in a Boston Massacre oration of 1777 by a lawyer named Benjamin Hichborn. The right of every citizen to reason freely concerning political questions, Hichborn maintained, had "nature for its source." He then proceeded to define civil liberty as "not 'a government by laws' made agreeable to charters, bills of rights or compacts, but a power existing in the people at large at any time, for any cause, or for no cause, but their own sovereign pleasure, to alter or annihilate both the mode and essence of any former government, and adopt a new one in its stead."[62] Here certainly was a challenge to proponents of positive law, but it was also a departure from the natural rights tradition to which New Englanders had been accustomed. For if political action could be undertaken for "any cause," or for "no cause," the "fixed principles" of natural law were no longer rhetorically functional in the public forum. This loss of relevance was one sign marking the advent of modern democratic politics in America.

The Legal and Religious Context of Natural Rights Theory: A Comment

Stanley N. Katz

Stephen Botein's essay is in the best tradition of historical revisionism. He resuscitates the argument from natural rights in understanding the movement toward the American Revolution at a time when it had begun to look as though the natural rights argument in general, and John Locke in particular, had been altogether rejected by historians.[1]

Carl Becker's *Declaration of Independence* and Randolph G. Adams' *Political Ideas of the American Revolution,*[2] with their almost simultaneous publication in 1922, established the framework in which the intellectual history of the Revolution would be understood for nearly fifty years. Reduced to essentials, their argument was that the colonists initially complained that the British Parliament was depriving them of their rights as Englishmen, but expressed confidence in the fairness and impartiality of the Crown. When by 1776, however, it was clear that not even the king would support their constitutional claims, and it became necessary "to dissolve the political bands" which connected them to their English brethren, the Americans resorted to a higher standard of political obligation—"the laws of nature and of nature's God."[3] The intellectual history of the Revolution was, then, the story of a progression from claims of English common law rights, to equal rights within an empire of Englishmen, and finally to an even higher law, the law of nature. For four decades variations on this view were the staple of American history courses, generally based upon Samuel Eliot Morison's edition of source materials, *Sources and Documents Illustrating the American Revolution, 1764-1788,* published a year after Becker and Adams in 1923.[4]

It is not surprising that these three books appeared shortly after the high point of Wilsonian idealism in an era of international appeal to the rights of mankind following the euphoria of Versailles. At any rate, the view was not seriously challenged until 1941, when Philip Davidson suggested in *Propaganda and the American Revolution* that the Patriots' ideas ought not to be taken seriously in themselves, but ought simply to be seen as ingenious attempts at popular persuasion.[5] There matters stood until the publication of Bernard Bailyn's *Ideological Origins of the American Revolution* in 1967 and Gordon S. Wood's *Creation of the American Republic* in 1969.[6]

Bailyn and Wood, along with many fine historians who have followed in their path, rejected the Lockean natural rights tradition as the core of Revolutionary rhetoric, and placed the origin of American political radicalism in a more indigenous and political English tradition—that of the early eighteenth-century opposition to the Hanoverian regime. Following the lead of Caroline Robbins,[7] Bailyn traced the impact of English radical opposition ideas of both the right (Bolingbroke)[8] and left (Trenchard and Gordon)[9] on American political ideology, and showed how the opposition critique of court administration came to have startling pertinence as a description of the American colonies' relationship to imperial authority. It was Bailyn's thesis that these ideas had a dramatically radicalizing effect on Americans of the later eighteenth century, so that in some sense English opposition ideology actually caused the Revolution. It is not necessary at this point to describe the brilliance of Bailyn's presentation, or the grandeur of vision with which Wood applied a similar perspective to the reinterpretation of the entire late-eighteenth-century period of American history. The fact is that the Bailyn-Wood view has tended to sweep all before it, at least insofar as the intellectual history of the American Revolution is concerned.

Curiously, however, neither the 1920's nor the 1960's interpretations took *religious* ideas seriously as a component of American opposition ideology. The classic argument for the impact of Puritan ideas on the Revolution was put forward as early as 1928 by Alice Mary Baldwin in *The New England Clergy and the American Revolution.*[10] While Professor Bailyn made a belated gesture toward recognizing the role of clergymen in the Revolutionary tradition,[11] most recent discussion of religion has been either in the context of identifying Puritan clergymen who espoused doctrines of political contract (Jonathan Mayhew) or Loyalist clerics in the South.[12] The one substantial deviation from this essentially secular tradition was the work of Alan E. Heimert, *Religion and the American Mind from the Great Awakening to the Revolution* (1966).[13] Heimert located the essence of American democratic ideas in the conservative-revivalist tradition of Protestantism which found its moment of greatest intensity in the era of the Great Awakening. Heimert's long, difficult, and rather perverse book has never received the serious attention it deserves; nor has sufficient interest been shown about the impact of religious ideas in what was, after all, still an intensely religious society. It may be that Perry Miller has so firmly convinced us of Puritanism's decline by the turn of the eighteenth century that we tend to forget that a preponderance of Americans until very recently always considered themselves to be practicing Protestants.[14] Political puritanism is a tradition worth re-examining, and this is one of the original contributions of Botein's paper.

A second element, also noted by Botein, which has tended to be ignored by historians of the Revolution, is the *legal* content of the Revolutionary debate. Here again, there is an early scholarly tradition originating in the 1920's, which became obscure and was ultimately rejected by the Bailyn school. The leading book here, published it might be noted in 1923, is Charles H. McIlwain's *The American Revolution: A Constitutional Interpretation*, which linked the natural rights arguments of Becker and Adams with an understanding of and an appreciation for the British constitutional tradition of the sixteenth and seventeenth centuries.[15] McIlwain attempted to show how Revolutionary eighteenth-century American political claims could be identified with those of the opponents of Stuart tyranny in seventeenth-century England. At the same time, and perhaps unwisely, he argued that the colonists were correct in their constitutional debates with imperial authorities, a view which was seriously and persuasively challenged by Robert Livingston Schuyler in 1929 in *Parliament and the British Empire*.[16]

The early 1930's witnessed the publication of a number of excellent books, noted by Botein, elaborating the role of "higher law" ideas in the early American constitutional tradition.[17] This scholarship treated the constitutional aspects of the Revolutionary debate as a subordinate set of problems of natural law and natural rights,[18] with the result that the existence of a specifically legal tradition has tended to become either forgotten or confused with the "higher law" discussion. Bailyn tends to ignore the legal side of political ideology, and though Gordon Wood is quite sensitive to the larger aspects of the problem,[19] it is only in the recent work of legal historians that the subject has been reopened.

The most noteworthy books are George Dargo's *Roots of the Republic: A New Perspective on Early American Constitutionalism* (1974); two recent books by law professor John Phillip Reid, *In a Defiant Stance: The Conditions of Law in Massachusetts Bay, the Irish Comparison and the Coming of the American Revolution* (1977), and *In a Rebellious Spirit: The Argument of Facts, the Liberty Riot and the Coming of the American Revolution* (1979); and the superb edition of *The Legal Papers of John Adams* edited by Kinvin Wroth and Hiller Zobel (1965).[20] Ironically, the two outstanding recent works of legal history which cover this period honor the Revolution by treating it as though it had no impact on the history of American law: William E. Nelson, *The Americanization of the Common Law* (1975), and Morton J. Horwitz, *The Transformation of American Law, 1780–1860* (1977).[21] Reid, in particular, has led the way in demonstrating how the technically legal arguments of the Revolutionaries can be assessed, and indeed his most recent book suggests that American Revolutionary rhetoric be discounted since much of it is written in the style of a legal "brief," the nature of which is to exaggerate argument for persuasive purpose within a self-consciously adversarial process. The revival of the tradition of legal history reminds us, at the very least, that Americans characteristically couched their Revolutionary appeals in intensely legal terms. Whether it was legal grievances or legal instincts that *caused* the movement for separation is, however, quite a different question.

It is the very great virtue of Botein's essay that it brings together the religious and legal traditions which have long been submerged in the historiography of the American Revolution. There is no doubt in my mind that he is correct in arguing for the strength and persistence of the natural rights tradition in eighteenth-century New England, and in finding the origins of this tradition in both the religious and legal cultures of the society. No one who has read a great many of the sermons or examined the political controversy of the era can have failed to note the prevalence of natural rights arguments, and I suspect our difficulty is that having run across them so often we take them for granted. Botein certainly does not. Furthermore, I find his argument that the natural rights tradition provided a *lingua franca* of political opposition quite persuasive.

My concern is whether New England religious and legal traditions do not in themselves adequately explain the frequent references to natural rights and natural law. If so, the natural rights language may have more rhetorical than causative importance. The religious theme of "withdrawal and reassociation" which Botein elaborates near the end of his paper is a wonderfully evocative expression of the religious tradition, and one which rings true. It is a way of linking the eighteenth century with the seventeenth century that makes good historical and intuitive sense. The same might be said for the legal tradition. Botein tends to abstract the legal tradition in a way that makes him sound more like Coke than Blackstone, and I am tempted to think that it is the mundane (or, if you will, common law) legal tradition that accounts for the reactions Botein describes.

It is, after all, primarily the notion of "contract" at law which Botein finds central to the legal tradition. There is no doubt that this is so, but of course the idea of contract was near the core of almost every aspect of eighteenth-century Anglo-American thought. I am intrigued when Botein dramatizes the pertinence of the contractual conception by adverting to the binding contractual terms which linked ministers to their parishes in eighteenth-century New England, and thus formed the basis for pastoral authority in the society. He is clearly correct in his analysis, but one need not move away from the common law in order to explain it. Indeed legal conceptions of contract have more explanatory power than theories of higher law relationships.[22]

Anyone who is familiar, for instance, with the Boyer-Nissenbaum interpretation of the origins of witchcraft in Salem will recall their account of the contractual disputes between Salem village and its succession of three ministers, James Bayley, George Burroughs, and Samuel Parris.[23] Boyer and Nissenbaum contend persuasively that the long history of legal dispute over the terms of pastoral authority in Salem was a critical element in upsetting the political stability of the village. A similar process was at work in almost all other areas of New England. A cursory glance, for instance, at the recently edited records of Plymouth County in Massachusetts Bay reveals several instances of contractual dispute between towns and their ministers.[24] A 1769 dispute uses language which makes Botein's point perfectly. A minister, Ivory Hovey, complained to the General Sessions that for the past year he had not been voted any payment by his parish in Rochester, and, being "reduced to great straits and difficulties," he pleaded with the court for relief.

The parish responded that they ought not to be so obligated, since from the time of Hovey's ordination in 1740 they had "always comfortably supported him agreeable to their contract made with him at the time of his settlement in the ministry amongst them." They contended, however, that acting upon the advice of an ecclesiastical council in 1768, "by mutual compact an agreement between him and said precinct the said original contract was dissolved and he separated and discharged from his pastoral relation, to said precinct and church . . . ."[25] All of Botein's central themes are here: contract, breach, separation, and withdrawal. One can understand the controversy in quite ordinary legal terms, however, without rising to the level of natural rights conceptions. The people of Rochester clearly thought that their relationship to their minister was defined and limited by the terms of their written contract with him; when they had a legal (even technical) ground for breaching the contract, they felt free to do so, and they expected the courts of the county to support their claims. This attitude can be, and was, generalized to political theory, but my own feeling is that the political debate moves from legal-constitutional rhetoric to the higher plane of political theory rather late in the colonial day, and at a time when "higher law" arguments are more rhetorically than legally useful. Insofar as the "higher law" argument was legally necessary, it was because the authority of the colonial legal system was characteristically seen as derivative from that of the mother country. Once the imperial bond was called into question, the colonists immediately needed a new theoretical basis on which to re-establish a legal regime.

This comment only begins to suggest the importance of Botein's revisionism, which provides such an elegant mode of synthesis for the New England intellectual tradition, and for the relationship of that tradition to its English original. From this perspective one is par-ticularly struck by the pertinence of seventeenth-century American concern for "the rights of Englishmen," as has been so well argued by David S. Lovejoy in the *Glorious Revolution in America* (1972).[26] Whether or not the Glorious Revolution in America had any true social roots, and I doubt that it did, the colonists availed themselves of a sort of immaculate reception of the constitutional benefits of the Civil War and the Glorious Revolution, and this became a tradition which sustained them throughout much of the eighteenth century. When after mid-century the Anglo-American legal system no longer seemed to protect the rights of Englishmen, they indeed did turn to natural law-natural rights arguments in order to locate a core legal and constitutional tradition which would protect them in the manner that the British constitution previously had been thought to do. Then, as Botein suggests and Gordon Wood has demonstrated,[27] the Americans crystallized their new conception of rights in a written constitutional scheme which served to specify and protect their liber-ties at the same time that it limited the radically democratic preten-sions of popular sovereignty ideas which had emerged during the Revolutionary era.

It can thus be seen how a long legal tradition in New England em-phasized the centrality of the rights of individuals in the constitu-tional system, and how that continuous concern led to reformulation of larger constitutional ideas in the face of changing imperial political circumstances. The rights of Englishmen were discovered to be the rights protected by the common law. The common law was, under the pressure of the separation crisis, identified with a hallowed legal-religious tradition of natural rights, and the new-old conception was embedded in the truly novel American idea of constitutionalism. If this sounds like McIlwain redivivus, so be it.

*

The Pattern of Factional Development in Pennsylvania, New York, and Massachusetts, 1682–1776

Marc Egnal

Scholars have taken two approaches to factional struggles in early America.[1] One approach is institutional, and most often focuses on the ability of the royal governor to deal with groups of dissident colonists. Such studies usually are restricted to a single colony and to a limited span of years.[2] The other approach is more broadly interpretative and extracts from the "rampant factionalism" of colonial America a transcendent theme, such as the rise of the assemblies or the development of a commonwealth ideology. The second school typically surveys several colonies and ascribes higher goals to no one faction but rather underscores the opportunism of the "outs" and "ins" who by turns furthered or retarded a larger campaign.[3] With few exceptions, works produced from either viewpoint share the assumption that colonial factions were short-lived, lacked coherence, and were held together simply by a desire for office rather than by any profounder interest or world view.[4] This paper questions such an assumption and argues that factions in Pennsylvania, New York, and Massachusetts were long-lived and coherent, and more specifically, that the parties which emerged in each colony by the 1740's continued until Independence and underlay the choice of loyalties in the Revolutionary crisis.

Long-term changes in the economy and a series of imperial wars together defined three periods of factional development between the end of the seventeenth century and 1776. The first era, which began in the 1680's or 1690's and ended by 1715, was marked by the vigorous clash of opposing groups. This period reflected the problems and opportunities associated with the exigencies of war and several decades of rapid economic expansion. The second phase, corresponding to a period of slower growth and an absence of armed conflict with the French, lasted from 1715 to 1740.[5] These years were characterized by the muting of partisan passions, although New York deviated from the pattern in the 1730's. The third period—the major focus of this essay—lasted from 1740 to 1776 and was dominated by the conflicts with France, Spain, and eventually Britain. The party divisions formed during this third era had roots traceable, for Massachusetts, back to the 1690's, and for New York, to the 1720's. But only after 1740 did party politics in the three colonies clearly turn on the same issues: territorial expansion and imperial regulation. These party lines endured, enabling leaders in one colony to share the perspectives of those in another—an essential precondition for Revolutionary cooperation—and also forming the polarities which came to be called Patriot and Tory.

The first two periods of party development, roughly 1685-1715 and 1715-40, in Pennsylvania, New York, and Massachusetts contrasted sharply: during the first, local elites fought to direct a burgeoning economy, while during the second, growth slackened and party feuds waned. Pennsylvania's politics conformed to this paradigm. Between the 1680's and about 1715 two prosperous Quaker groups battled for control of local institutions. One faction, which we may term the Quaker Grandees, held a firm grip on the Yearly Meeting and could count on support from wealthy Chester and Bucks county farmers like Caleb Pusey and Phineas Pemberton, and from a number of Philadelphia's Quaker merchants, including Anthony Morris and Joseph Redman. The opposing faction, which may be called the Quaker Dissidents, drew its strength from the landowners of Philadelphia County and from the city's overseas traders, including both Quakers like Joseph Fisher and Robert Turner, and non-Quakers such as Patrick Robinson. The Dissidents, far more than the Grandees, attracted adherents among the non-Quakers and lower orders.[6]

Between the 1680's and 1715 the Quaker Grandees gradually established themselves as the dominant faction. Before 1700 the

Grandees, led by Thomas Lloyd, fought a two-front war, opposing the Proprietor as well as the Dissidents. The Grandees, for example, battled with William Penn over his land policy, particularly over his demand for quitrents, and at the same time sought to impose their own tax scheme and to restrict the political role of non-Quakers. Lloyd and his associates led the opposition to a succession of governors in the 1680's and 1690's, while the Dissidents welcomed these executives and willingly served them. In 1700 the Quaker Grandees reached an accord with Penn, and during the next decade and a half were able to establish their dominance in all branches of government. The accord reflected the Proprietor's recognition of the strength of this entrenched Quaker faction and his willingness to trade points of privilege for financial assistance. The Grandees' dominance of appointive offices now was assured. Members of this faction, many of whom—like Pusey and Pemberton—were old opponents of Penn, and some of whom—such as James Logan and Andrew Hamilton—were newly recruited Proprietary men, were placed on the bench and in the council chamber. The Quaker Dissidents opposed the Grandees after 1700 much as they had before, but now they no longer had an ally in the executive office. The strength of this faction was on the wane, and during the second decade of the eighteenth century the Dissidents, one by one, made their separate peace with the dominant Grandees. By Penn's death in 1718 Pennsylvania's first set of factional wars had come to an end.[7]

The problems accompanying the next, slow-paced period of growth, from 1715 to the early 1740's, tended to unite Pennsylvanians rather than to factionalize them. Hard times fostered a noisy dispute between 1721 and 1725 over the wisdom of issuing paper money. But most notable in this debate was the small size of the opposition to bills of credit and the broad consensus favoring more paper currency. Although Isaac Norris and James Logan, both former Grandees, condemned the currency issues of 1723, a potent coalition of other Grandees, like Jeremiah Langhorne and Anthony Morris, and former Dissidents, like David Lloyd and Francis Rawle, supported the measure, as did Governors Sir William Keith (1718-26) and Patrick Gordon (1726-36). More directly linked to the earlier divisions was

Keith's attempt in 1726 to form his own party in opposition to his successor, Patrick Gordon. Keith worked to revivify the Quaker Dissidents, but his efforts failed and he left the province in 1728 a defeated man.[8] The last years of the 1720's and the 1730's were free of partisan battles. In 1729, £30,000 of paper money was struck with little debate. Only when the issue of defense was raised in 1740 did Pennsylvanians again flock to party standards.[9]

The factions that emerged in New York after 1689 were long-lived and cohesive, as in Pennsylvania, but unlike the Quaker Colony this first period of strife was followed in the 1720's by a new set of struggles with imperial issues in the forefront. From 1689 until about 1715 New York's factional wars pitted Leislerians against anti-Leislerians and turned on the highly unequal way that wealth and political power were distributed. New York's rapid growth during the last decades of the century was characterized above all by the award of enormous estates to the governors' favorites; between 1680 and 1700 most of the colony's great holdings—Cortlandt Manor, Livingston Manor, Highland Patent, Morrisania, Philipsborough, and lesser fiefdoms—were carved out. The Leislerians who seized power in 1689 were neither poor men nor levelers; they were ambitious individuals of moderate wealth like Jacob Leisler, Samuel Staats, and Abraham DePeyster, who had been excluded from the spoils so lavishly bestowed on others. Arrayed against them was the colony's elite, including Nicholas Bayard, Robert Livingston, and Frederick Philipse.[10]

Although Jacob Leisler's brief reign ended in March 1691, the conflict between his followers and the colony's aristocracy continued for over two decades. The anti-Leislerians profited from the extreme partisanship of Governor Benjamin Fletcher (1692-98), but they were thoroughly frightened by the intentions of the next governor, the Earl of Bellomont (1698-1701). Lord Bellomont decided that the accumulation of land in so few hands was dangerous to the colony's growth and to the royal prerogative; with the help of the Leislerians in the Assembly he secured the annulment of the Mohawk Patent, one of Fletcher's most extravagant awards. He wrote to his superiors asking for assistance in his attack on the other large landed estates, "for

I am a little jealous I shall not have strength enough in the Assembly of New York to break them."[11] Although Bellomont died in 1701, the Leislerian-controlled legislature, undaunted and perhaps less conscious of its limitations than the governor had been, adopted a bill to confiscate Livingston Manor. Lord Cornbury (1702-08) checked these designs, but did little to quiet factional feuds. That was the work of Robert Hunter (1710-19), who engineered a broad compromise: the anti-Leislerians were confirmed in their estates and political supremacy, while selected Leislerians were installed in office and rewarded with public funds. Thus Hunter appointed the Leislerians Staats, DePeyster, and Robert Walters to council; and with the Debt Acts of 1714 and 1717 he disbursed £45,000 both to Leislerians, such as Jacob Leisler, Jr., and to anti-Leislerians, like Robert Livingston and Philip Schuyler. One set of conflicts had come to an end.[12]

But another set of factions, one which divided the victorious anti-Leislerians and foreshadowed later divisions, formed during the period of slow economic growth between 1715 and 1740. Parties emerged as New Yorkers argued over provincial policy toward the hinterland and particularly toward the dealings with New France in which English and Dutch goods were exchanged for hides. The arrival of Governor William Burnet (1720-28), who called for firm measures against the French, precipitated the schism. One group, led in the early 1720's by Adolph Philipse, Stephen DeLancey, and Peter Schuyler, wanted to maintain a strict neutrality toward the French and so protect the flourishing commerce between Albany and Montreal. Opposed to Philipse's party was a faction headed by Lewis Morris and Robert Livingston that called for the interdiction of trade with Canada and the extension of English influence to embrace dealings with the Great Lakes Indians. Although a variety of issues would keep the two factions at loggerheads, self-interest played an important role in the initial split: Philipse, DeLancey, and Schuyler were involved personally in the Albany-Montreal trade, whereas Morris and Livingston stood apart from it.[13]

In the 1730's the two factions, hitherto mere cliques of rival politicians, acquired popular followings, and gradually those broad divisions which would characterize New York politics in later years were elaborated. The partisan behavior of Governor William Cosby (1732–36) riled New Yorkers; among other actions, he removed Lewis Morris from the chief justice's chair and elevated James DeLancey, and he had Morrisite printer John Peter Zenger jailed for libel. The response to these acts revealed the fault lines that ran beneath New York's political soil. The Morris-Livingston party received support from the large landowners of the upper Hudson Valley, including the Van Rensselaers, Beekmans, and Livingstons, whose economic well-being increasingly was linked to the down-river staple trade and who shared a desire for a firm policy against the French and Indians.[14] The Morrisites also could rely on former Leislerians, such as the DePeysters and Gouverneurs, and on a number of Presbyterians, merchants, lawyers, and New York City artisans.[15] The DeLancey-Philipse group dominated the Long Island counties and Staten Island, and seems to have been stronger among Anglicans and New York City's upper classes. These divisions were not rigid ones, but they were evident on a number of crucial issues and in Assembly votes (recorded after 1737), and would underlie factional disputes after 1740. Furthermore, the enduring tensions between dissimilar groups in New York help explain why the peaceful, economically depressed decades of the 1720's and 1730's were a time of partisan turmoil in New York but of relative political calm in Pennsylvania and Massachusetts.[16]

Like Pennsylvania and New York, the Bay Colony underwent two periods of factional conflict between 1690 and 1740, with the first era marked by brisker economic growth and more bitter partisanship than the second. Throughout these years, and indeed until the end of the colonial period, Massachusetts politics was characterized by three factions. From 1690 to 1715 these parties, each little more than a congeries of like-minded individuals, quarreled over defense spending and the money supply. One group, the expansionists, enthusiastically supported the attempts to assert control over Maine and the coastal waters, and favored a moderate increase in the province's currency. This faction, which included merchants and liberal clerics like Wait Winthrop, Thomas Brattle, and Penn Townshend, applauded those governors who took a firm stand on defense and criticized the executives who did not.[17] A second group, the non-expansionists, was led by Boston traders and old-line ministers such as Thomas Hutchinson, Sr., Samuel Sewall, and Cotton Mather. Although not pacifists, they were more ready than the expansionists to find fault with the colony's campaigns against the French; they were also hard-money advocates.[18] The third faction drew its strength from Boston's lower ranks and the poorer agricultural communities; of two minds on the issue of military spending, this group was staunchly inflationist. Among its leaders were Elisha Cooke, Sr. and Jr., and Oliver Noyes.[19]

In 1714 and 1715 the differences among the three factions were brought into sharp relief by a dispute over the future of the colony's money supply. Thomas Hutchinson, in his *History of Massachusetts-Bay,* described the positions taken:

> Three parties were formed, one very small, which were for drawing in the paper bills and depending upon silver and gold currency. Mr. [Thomas] Hutchinson [Sr.], one of the members for Boston, was among the most active of this party. . . .
>
> Another party was very numerous. These had projected a private bank. . . . There was nothing more in it, than issuing bills of credit. . . . Three of the representatives of Boston, Mr. [Elisha] Cooke [Jr.], . . . Mr. [Oliver] Noyes . . . and Mr. [William] Payne, were the supporters of the party. . . .
>
> A third party, though very opposite to the private bank yet were no enemies to bills of credit.[20]

After much debate, the compromise position set forth by the "third party," the expansionists, was adopted: £ 50,000 was issued by a government-controlled bank, which was carefully and conservatively supervised.[21]

Between 1715 and 1740 the earlier divisions persisted in Massachusetts, although during this period of slower economic growth and relative political tranquility the three parties resolved themselves into two groups. Beginning in 1717 the Bay Colony waged war against the native peoples in Maine. Governor Samuel Shute (1716-23), advised by non-expansionists like Samuel Sewall, was reluctant to commit the province's resources to the conflict; his policies were opposed by the expansionists and by the "country" or "popular" party (as Elisha Cooke, Jr., and Oliver Noyes' faction sometimes was called), which saw the war as a good excuse for increasing the currency supply. William Dummer (1723-28) prosecuted the Indian war vigorously and gained Shute's enemies as his allies.[22] With the end of the fighting in 1725 "the temper of the house was much changed," and politics became calmer though never placid.[23] The two upper-class factions coalesced, it appears, in opposition to the popular party and regularly were able to elect William Dudley as Speaker. In 1727 a Bostonian stated firmly: "We have at present two parties, Dudley and Cooke. . . ."[24] Governor William Burnet (1728-29) drew his support from Dudley's followers, although even these men resisted his demands for a permanent revenue. Trying a different tack, Burnett's successor, Jonathan Belcher (1730-41), began his administration by striking a deal with the popular party: his patronage in return for a generous salary. But, as Hutchinson notes, "the prerogative men were Mr. Belcher's old friends," and the accord with Elisha Cooke's coterie was short-lived.[25] Belcher spent his last years in office fighting the popular party's attempt to revive the land bank scheme first proposed in 1714.[26]

In sum, the parties that formed in Pennsylvania, New York, and Massachusetts between the 1680's and 1740 were cohesive groups that in most cases endured for several decades. Furthermore, in the two colonies—New York and Massachusetts—where imperial issues were of some importance before 1740, the pattern of factional politics foreshadowed the alignments evident in subsequent decades. But the divisions formed during the first two periods of party development differed from those that emerged during the third era. These early parties fought for the most part over local issues and lacked the broad ideological underpinnings that characterized factions after 1740.

The divisions of the third period of party development, from the 1740's to Independence, emerged from conflicts in Pennsylvania, New York, and Massachusetts over the course of empire in the New World. Two issues predominated. Between 1740 and 1763 Americans argued over the wisdom of supporting the British campaigns against the French and Spanish; after 1763 they debated the merits of resistance to British policies. Looked at together, these questions divided the colonists into two camps. One faction viewed America as a territorially and economically expansionist state, and asserted the colonies' claims to western lands and maritime trading rights in opposition to the policies of France, Spain, and eventually Great Britain. The other faction was content for America to grow more slowly within a London-centered empire that provided defense and direction. This party was reluctant, before 1763, to endorse warlike measures unless colonial forces were subsidized by Britain, and was hesitant, after 1763, to oppose the mother country's decrees. Put in other terms, in each province the party which voted for military spending during King George's War and the French and Indian War later supported the Patriot cause, while the faction which opposed preparedness at mid-century became Tory or reluctantly patriotic in its sympathies. Although the parties went by different names in each colony, we may call the first group the expansionists and the second the non-expansionists.

In Pennsylvania the clash between those who endorsed an aggressive American imperium and those who envisaged the future in more static terms underlay partisan politics between 1740 and 1776. In the 1740's and 1750's the expansionists drew their support from the Scotch-Irish farmers in the western counties and from wealthy Philadelphians. In the capital the party's adherents included Anglicans such as Thomas Willing and Robert Morris, Presbyterians like William Allen, and a few individuals not closely identified with any sect, like James Hamilton and Benjamin Franklin. More than any other Pennsylvanian at mid-century, Franklin articulated the expansionist outlook. Franklin's bold conception of an American imperium was evident in his advocacy of firm measures against the French and Indians, his call for a colony in the Ohio Valley—the area, he observed in 1754, "must undoubtedly ... become a populous and powerful dominion"— and his assertion of American rights whenever he felt that Britain was "extending the prerogative beyond its due bounds."[27] During these same years the strength of the non-expansionists lay with Philadelphia's Quaker community, including John Kinsey and Isaac Norris, and with the English, German, and

Welsh farmers of Philadelphia, Bucks, and Chester counties. Philadelphia's lower orders were divided in their loyalties.[28]

From 1740 to 1755 the expansionists, with the exception of a few individuals, could be equated with Pennsylvania's Proprietary party, while the non-expansionists were coterminous with the Quaker party. The outbreak of war between England and Spain in 1739 and the efforts of Governor George Thomas to enlist indentured servants and others for the British forces precipitated the divisions.[29] The newly formed Quaker party easily dominated the thirty-six-seat Assembly because of an apportionment which allowed the party strongholds of Bucks, Philadelphia, and Chester counties eight representatives each. This faction, under the leadership of Speaker John Kinsey, defined a cautious position toward King George's War. It opposed a militia act and resisted Governor Thomas' efforts to recruit soldiers, but it voted modest sums to provision the forces at Louisbourg and to assist an expedition against Canada.[30] For the expansionists, these efforts were not enough, especially as fear of an invasion by French privateers mounted. Benjamin Franklin, one of the few politically active Philadelphians to maintain a stance of nonpartisanship toward the Quaker and Proprietary factions, worked with other expansionists—almost all Proprietary party men—to establish a volunteer militia in 1747. With the return of peace in 1748 party conflict eased, but many Pennsylvanians and most upper-class Philadelphians remained associated with the Quaker or Proprietary factions through membership in exclusive, partisan social clubs and civic organizations.[31]

Between 1755 and 1764 a group of Pennsylvania expansionists, led by Franklin, allied themselves with the more moderate non-expansionists in the Quaker party, thereby tempering the pacifism of the Quaker party and assuring that faction's ascendancy during the French and Indian War. Braddock's defeat in western Pennsylvania in July 1755 and the ensuing discussion in Parliament of a test act to exclude Friends from Pennsylvania's government put pressure on the Quaker party to adopt a more aggressive policy. At this juncture, Franklin abandoned his factional neutrality and joined the Quaker party. He did so, in part, so he could work from within the dominant faction for a militia act, mutiny act, and large defense appropriations. The moderates in the Quaker party, confronted with the choice of disenfranchisement or military preparedness, grudgingly followed Franklin's lead.[32] The printer's bold move produced a noticeable change in the personnel of the Proprietary and Quaker factions. A number of expansionists, including Charles Thomson and Daniel Roberdeau, joined the Quaker party along with Franklin, while a "stiff rump" of pacifist Friends disassociated themselves from the Quaker party and went into a principled opposition.[33] Franklin had acted, it would appear, from a second motive: his desire to make Pennsylvania a royal colony and so make possible his accession as governor. At Franklin's behest, the new-modeled Quaker party took up the cause of a royal charter, a campaign which climaxed in the Assembly resolves of 1764.[34]

During the dozen years before Independence the division between expansionists and non-expansionists lay at the heart of Revolutionary politics in Pennsylvania. Those expansionists like Benjamin Franklin who had supported the Quaker party during the war now joined with the Proprietary men to protest British policies.[35] Playing an increasing role among the expansionists were the Presbyterians. Some contemporaries singled out these Calvinists as a separate, radical party, but in fact Presbyterian expansionists, like George Bryan and John Mease, worked alongside Anglicans, such as George Clymer and Thomas Willing, as well as with Patriots of Quaker origin like Thomas Mifflin and John Dickinson, to lead the Whig resistance.[36] The non-expansionists were more reluctant to oppose Britain; during the depths of the depression of the 1760's, however, conservative Quakers readily supported non-consumption and non-importation.[37] After 1770 the outlook of both upper-class parties, the Proprietary-Presbyterian and the Quaker, was transformed by the growing involvement of the lower orders in the Revolutionary movement. Most of the non-expansionists adhered to the principles they had long followed and became Loyalists. In addition, a significant group of expansionists, including the Allens and Joseph Swift, who were frightened by the demands of artisans and western farmers, cast their lot with the Tories. But the leadership of the Patriot cause,

which was never wholly wrested from upper-class hands, remained
with the expansionists, many of whom, like Franklin, Roberdeau, and
Willing, had evinced over the course of several decades a consistent
faith in a dynamic, sovereign America.[38]

In New York, as in Pennsylvania, a division over the approach to
empire underlay political struggles between 1740 and 1776. The clash
between expansionists and non-expansionists in New York, however,
unlike that in the Quaker Colony, had its origins in the pre-1740
period. Imperial issues had separated some Yorkers in the 1720's, and
in the 1730's the fissure had widened; subsequent party battles only
confirmed this split. The expansionists drew their strength chiefly
from the wealthy landowners of the upper Hudson Valley, including
the Livingstons, Van Rensselaers, and Beekmans, and from New
York City merchants and lawyers like the Livingstons, Van Cort-
landts, and Alexanders. This faction also was backed by the Morrises
of Westchester County and by the representatives of the west Hudson small farmers, particularly those of Ulster County. The non-
expansionists received support from the Long Islanders, from the
small farmers of Richmond and Orange counties, and from landowners of the lower Hudson, like the Philipses. Most significantly,
the party could rely on an influential group of New York merchants
including the DeLanceys, Waltons, and Crugers. Although at times
political allegiances were fluid, these divisions were long-lived and remained at the heart of partisan struggles during this era.[39]

Between 1740 and 1748 the conflict of expansionists and non-
expansionists was evident in New York despite the heavy-handed
assertiveness of Governor George Clinton (1743-53), which eventually created a broad alliance of politicians opposed to the executive.
Clinton's first years in New York were calm ones. His able
predecessor, George Clarke (1736-43), had reconciled feuding factions, and the continuation of peace with New France in 1743 and
1744 allowed Clinton to avoid divisive requests for larger appropriations. Moreover, Clinton gained a powerful ally by drawing close to
James DeLancey, a non-expansionist who was linked through family
ties to the trade with Montreal. DeLancey was willing to support the
governor's moderate defense program in return for a hand in the

distribution of patronage and for influence over other policies.[40] But
with the French attack on Saratoga in November 1745 and the escala-
tion of fighting, political tranquility was ended. Clinton now demanded funds for an expedition against Canada, and DeLancey broke with
him to become the leader of an outspoken opposition ("the Faction,"
Clinton called it).[41] Clinton, foolishly, did not shore up his support
among those expansionists like the Livingstons and Morrises who
rallied to his aggressive war policies, often abusing them as bitterly
as he did the DeLanceyites.[42] The governor's hostility to the non-
expansionists and his mismanagement of the expansionists impeded
but did not check the colony's contribution to defense. In 1746 and
1747 the expansionists in the legislature voted over £70,000 for the
war effort.[43]

Between 1749 and 1762 expansionists and non-expansionists in
New York battled over the merits of Governors Clinton and
DeLancey, the establishment of a college, and the French and Indian
War. During the second half of his administration Clinton endeavored
to strengthen his ties with those who shared his expansive view of
empire. He drew closer to James Alexander, William Smith, Sr., and
the Morrises, although few politicians supported the irascible governor with enthusiasm.[44] Clinton's departure in 1753 and the elevation
of James DeLancey (1753–55, 1757–60) to the post of acting governor
ended the loose coalition that had formed in opposition to the executive and made apparent once more that imperial views were the
basis of faction. In 1754 and 1755 the fight over whether King's College was to be non-denominational or Anglican fell generally along
party lines. Those who endorsed strong war measures sought a broad
base for the college; their more pacifistic opponents wanted to
preserve the prerogatives of the established church.[45] A similar division emerged during the first years of the French and Indian War
over the question of defense. Governor DeLancey, leader of the non-
expansionists, dragged his heels on aid for the British effort. Conse-
quently, William Shirley, who had been appointed commander in chief
after Braddock's death in 1755, by-passed DeLancey's followers and
turned to New York's expansionists for aid in securing supplies.
Beginning only in 1757, when Pitt encouraged the colonists with the

promise of lavish subventions, did New Yorkers of all persuasions readily back the war effort.[46] Party lines were evident, however, in votes on limiting Governor DeLancey's powers.[47]

When the Revolutionary movement began, long-held views of empire were at the core of partisan conflicts in New York, although the identification of the expansionists with the Patriots and the non-expansionists with the Loyalists was not fully apparent until 1769. In the mid-1760's two developments disrupted the pattern of New York politics. First, the deepening depression led merchants of both parties to support the political and economic protests against Britain. Captain James DeLancey and John Cruger were no less patriotic than their political opponents, Philip Livingston and Gerard Beekman.[48] Second, the uprising of tenant farmers in 1766, which was suppressed by British regulars, thoroughly frightened the great landed proprietors of the upper Hudson and made them reconsider—at least temporarily—their criticism of the mother country. Since these landowners comprised an important group within the expansionist faction, the patriotism of that party was tempered, and during the mid-1760's neither party could lay sole claim to the leadership of the Revolutionary movement.[49] By 1769 the economic downturn had eased, the outrages of the small farmers had subsided, and the Livingstons and DeLanceys (for so New Yorkers now often termed the expansionist and non-expansionist parties) had become, respectively, the Patriots and the Tories. The final choice of allegiances reflected a pattern that had been evident even before the 1740's. Despite worries about the restless "lower orders," most of the expansionists, including the Livingstons, Morrises, and Beekmans, supported the new American government, while non-expansionists like the DeLanceys, Philipses, and Crugers cast their lot with Great Britain.[50]

In Massachusetts, as in Pennsylvania and New York, expansionists and non-expansionists battled from 1740 to 1776; politics in the Bay Colony was complicated, however, by the presence of a third group—the "popular" party. This threefold division dated back to the seventeenth century. As in earlier decades, the expansionists drew their leadership from Boston's merchants and professional men—individuals such as the Hancocks and Bowdoins—and from the elites of

the smaller coastal communities. The expansionists shared a common
outlook not only on matters of defense but also on the currency question; they pursued a middle course between the non-expansionists,
who favored hard money, and the inflationary popular party. The second faction, the non-expansionists, received its most consistent support from traders and other men in the larger seaboard towns, particularly Boston, Salem, and Marblehead. Numbered among the
leaders of the party were the Hutchinsons and Olivers. But it was the
third group, the popular or country party, that gave Massachusetts
politics its unique cast; until the eve of Independence, this lower-class
faction had no counterpart in New York or Pennsylvania. The popular
party drew its strength from the artisans and lesser traders who held
sway at the Boston town meeting and from the poorer farmers whose
voices were dominant in a broad arc of towns about twenty-five miles
from the capital. James Allen, John Tyng, and Samuel Adams helped
guide this large, occasionally unruly constituency. The popular party
generally, but not unalterably, opposed defense spending in the
1740's and 1750's, and warmly supported an inflationary currency.
Between 1740 and 1776 no single party was dominant and the
colony's political battles were marked by a series of shifting coalitions.[51]

During King George's War Governor William Shirley (1741-57)
relied on the expansionists and a portion of the popular party to support an extensive program of military measures. Men with a bold vision of empire, like Thomas Cushing, Sr., helped the governor enlist
troops for the Caribbean campaigns, and other like-minded individuals, such as Thomas Hancock and James Otis, Sr., assisted
with the expedition against Louisbourg.[52] In addition, Shirley won
over key popular party men like Robert Hale and John Choate, who
applauded the governor's willingness to sign a series of wartime currency issues.[53] Shirley also received support from the "river gods" of
the Connecticut Valley, a powerful, local elite involved in land
speculation and military contracting; these men, rulers of Springfield,
Northampton, Hadley, and other river towns, formed a clique whose
interests meshed consistently with none of the factions in the eastern
part of the province.[54] The non-expansionists were critical of Shirley

during most of the war years. Men such as Theophilus Lillie and Benjamin Faneuil mistrusted the governor's readiness to authorize large emissions of currency and, like Thomas Hutchinson, who termed the Louisbourg expedition "rash," they felt that Shirley's military plans were fraught with unnecessary risks.[55]

Between 1748 and 1760 Governors Shirley and Thomas Pownall (1757-60) worked with several distinct coalitions drawn from the colony's three factions. With the end of King George's War, Shirley accepted the contractionist argument that the elimination of the colony's inflated currency was a necessity. He drew closer to the non-expansionists, whom he had battled during the war, and made Thomas Hutchinson his chief adviser.[56] The popular party, under the leadership of Bostonians James Allen and John Tyng, bitterly opposed Shirley's new policies, while the response of the expansionists to the governor's program ranged from James Otis, Sr.'s approval to Thomas Hancock's dissent.[57] Fighting resumed in 1754 and Shirley turned to his old expansionist allies like Thomas Hancock and James Otis, Sr., for help in securing and implementing defense measures.[58] But Shirley, who was appointed commander in chief in 1755, spent much of his time out of the colony, and the work of forging a wartime coalition was left to his successor, Thomas Pownall. The new executive successfully wooed expansionists like Hancock and James Bowdoin, and also gained the support of popular party men on a number of political issues. This lower-class faction bridled, however, at Pownall's military program.[59] The non-expansionists opposed the governor's ambitious wartime plans; Thomas Hutchinson, for example, was willing in 1758 to settle for "a peace if but just tolerable."[60] The "river gods" of western Massachusetts, ever pursuing their own course, supported defense measures but opposed Pownall on most other questions.[61]

During the decade and a half before Independence the cohesiveness and longevity of the three factions were evident despite a series of shifting alliances between the parties. Governor Francis Bernard (1760-69) hoped to establish his administration "on the broad bottom of a collation,"[62] and initially distributed patronage to both upper-class factions: to non-expansionists like Thomas Hutchinson and to expansionists such as the Hancocks and Otises.[63] But with the mounting protests against British policy, Bernard's "collation" dissolved, and by 1765 popular party men like Samuel Adams were working with expansionists such as John Hancock and Thomas Cushing in an unstable union often called the Friends of Liberty.[64] Thereafter the strongest support for Governor Barnard came from non-expansionists like the Hutchinsons and Olivers, and from the "river gods," who justly feared that the Revolutionary movement would endanger their control over local politics.[65] But the polarization of Massachusetts politics was not yet absolute. As in other colonies, during the depression of the 1760's merchants of various persuasions joined forces on specific economic measures.[66] Moreover, the Friends of Liberty, which bridged two dissimilar factions, was a fragile alliance. During 1771 and 1772, when the protests waned, expansionists like Hancock and Cushing responded to the blandishments of the new governor, Thomas Hutchinson (1769–74), and pulled away from their popular party allies.[67] The Patriot alliance re-emerged in 1773, however, called back into existence by quarrels between the governor and Assembly. In the Revolutionary crisis the expansionists, following the logic of their beliefs, supported Independence, just as the non-expansionists, equally consistent, opposed it. The popular party, which long had linked its struggles in Massachusetts to the battle against Britain, was ardently patriotic.[68]

It can be said in summary, then, that the factions which formed in colonial Pennsylvania, New York, and Massachusetts were cohesive, long-enduring groups that were characterized—particularly after 1740—by firmly held convictions. The coherence of party lines and the importance of the issue of expansion during the last decades of the colonial period suggest new approaches in our effort to understand the Revolution. The analysis of factional politics undertaken here indicates that the division of political leaders into Patriots and Loyalists was in significant degree a product of long-standing associations and allegiances. Furthermore, the consistency of word and deed exhibited by many colonists between 1740 and 1776 suggests that the effective ideology of the Revolutionaries was one of expansionism rather than of constitutional rights. The struggle against Britain was led by individuals who long had nurtured a vision of a growing, self-assertive America, and who concluded that their goals could be realized only in an independent nation.[69]

Empire and Faction: A Comment

Alison Gilbert Olson

In writing "The Pattern of Factional Development in Pennsylvania, New York, and Massachusetts, 1682–1776," Marc Egnal develops three points in particular. First, he has found expansion and inflation to be the major issues dividing political factions in the three colonies in the generation before the American Revolution. Second, he has found that those factions favoring expansion and inflation in the mid-eighteenth century also favored independence from Britain in 1776. Finally, he suggests that his hypothesis about Massachusetts, New York, and Pennsylvania may extend to other colonies as well; expansion in particular was everywhere an issue uniting parties and dividing the empire.

In emphasizing expansion as the paramount issue behind partisan attitudes, Egnal has provided us a strong lead in the search for new ways of looking at politics in the Revolutionary era. At the moment his work remains no more than a lead, because his concentration on the shifts and maneuvers of particular party chieftains has kept him from developing the argument against a larger background of imperial, provincial, and local politics. What is needed is a larger context for the study, one that will enable us to understand why expansion was such a broadly divisive issue in the quarter-century before the Revolution.

To begin, we must look at eighteenth-century British politics if we are to understand how the British came to adopt a series of stances guaranteed to infuriate Americans interested in expansion. Then we must examine the emergence at mid-century of a generation of colonial political leaders eager for the first time to build a power base in the colonies, rather than in England, and sufficiently committed to expansion to make it a major issue. We also need to look at the growing popular interest in provincial politics, and to ask why expansion

61

was an issue of concern to locals only now becoming aware of politics beyond their immediate neighborhoods. Then we must ask: Was expansion the *best* issue (not merely a good one) for explaining colonial alignments? How do we measure this? Can the divisions over expansion fairly be labeled political parties?[1] And finally, what are the larger implications of Egnal's conclusions for the study of Revolutionary politics? Clearly, a brief comment is not the place either to fill in the background in depth or answer these questions in detail; there is space enough only to suggest some general lines of inquiry.

One such line concerns the development of British restrictions on American expansion in the 1760's and 1770's. To the Americans, these restrictions appeared to result from a sudden abandonment of traditional British support for colonial growth; in reality, however, they represented a return to a century-old British concern about the dangers of inland colonial expansion, which had itself been temporarily put aside at mid-century.

Long-standing British anxieties about colonial expansion were manifold and well-grounded. Inland expansion meant the end of all hope of policing and defending the colonies with the British navy. It also meant increased expenses for defense and administration.[2] Moreover, inland expansion meant the endless proliferation of small villages, which in their rural isolation would develop an outlook different from the mercantile, cosmopolitan, and hence English-oriented, society of the seaboard. Perhaps most disturbing of all, expansion meant a new American psychology in revolt from the culture of Europe: European culture emphasized man's development toward greater perfectability within a sequential framework of time; frontier culture substituted instead the constant re-creation of the timeless frontier experience. To the English mind—as one can see from the Board of Trade's repeated emphasis on the need for an urban society in North America—this was a reversion to savagery.[3]

Among English politicians expansion was a practical concern, because it would tend either toward the multiplication of new colonies or the enlargement of old ones, and neither alternative was desirable. New colonies were a problem because the more legislatures a monarch had to deal with, the more thinly he divided his time and talent for distributing "influence," the only known way of managing an assembly in the eighteenth century. As J.G.A. Pocock has argued, the "management" of one legislature alone was a full-time job; the management of many legislatures would be so difficult that government might well get out of control. The enlargement of old colonies was also a problem. As population increased, so did the number of representatives in the colonial assemblies, and in British thinking large assemblies were harder to manage than small ones. Besides, the addition of an inland empire in the colonies simply multiplied the number of issues on which the government could be embarrassed in Parliament. However one looked at it, expansion meant problems for British politicians.[4]

Economically, inland colonies posed endless problems. "What could we gain by settling colonies in that part of the world?" wrote one contributor to the *Gentleman's Magazine* in 1754. "Colonies so distant from the sea, that we could never have any intercourse with them in the way of commerce? Colonies. . .whose very situation would put them under a necessity, and the fruitfulness of whose country would afford them the means of rivalling Great Britain in every article of its manufacturers."[5]

Finally, the British were all too aware of empires ruined by overexpansion. Rome, they often argued, had been swallowed up by her own colonies. Spain, too, had extended her empire too far: "Over colonized and hence went into decline" wrote the Duke of Bedford about that country.

All these worries were widely shared; they dated back at least to the late seventeenth century when Charles Davenant had suggested that "many empires have been ruined by too much enlarging their dominions,"[6] and when Governor Berkeley had precipitated rebellion in Virginia by ineffectively trying to limit expansion. But by the mid-eighteenth century a new element was introduced, as it became clear for the first time that continued westward expansion of the colonies would soon bring them to lands claimed by the French. Was it advisable to challenge the French in North America? A broad cross section of the British political nation, from radical journalists to conservative merchants and ministers of all factions, said "No"; a substantial wing of the government's mercantile advisers led by Sir John Barnard called the American frontier "a wild settlement, made in a country defenseless, open to the enemy, where there was scarce a possibility for us to succeed."[7] Even Dr. Shebbeare, the radical writer, called the Ohio territory "a distant and problematical advantage."[8]

There was, in short, widespread reluctance, for traditional reasons, to enter the Seven Years' War. Ministers were pushed into it by the pressures of a miscellaneous group of English political and mercantile leaders, including some traditionalists, who argued that the American conflict was simply a necessary extension of the European war.[9]

British support for American expansionists in the Seven Years' War obscured for the moment traditional British reluctance to encourage colonial expansion, but postwar policies returned gradually to the traditional line. The removal of the French threat, the expansion of American settlement to the limits of an area naturally defensible against the Indians, and the deep-seated British reluctance to assume trusteeship over native peoples all combined with a conviction that peaceful Indian relations were essential to stable colonial development, convincing many, indeed most, British politicians of the wisdom of returning to the old policy. Yet not all politicians agreed. Some were for letting the Americans press ahead and create their own western policies. Thus successive British ministries vacillated, according to the sentiments of members entrusted with the development of western policy, from attempts to establish a line beyond which settlement could not go (1763-68), to a reliance on American provincial governments to regulate their own frontiers (1763-74), to the attempted regulation of western territories from Canada in the Quebec Act of 1774. (The Quebec Act is, of course, essential to Egnal's argument; otherwise we are left asking why, if expansion became a divisive issue in the 1740's, it did not lead to revolution until 1776). American expansionists in their turn reacted to each ministerial shift, sometimes entertaining faint hopes of British support, sometimes despairing of it, ultimately giving up all attempts to work within the British system.[10]

If it is useful to develop Egnal's argument in the context of imperial politics, it is also useful to fit it into the context of a developing provincial leadership actively seeking popular issues at mid-century. Expansion was an appealing issue to colonial leaders who had abandoned hope of achieving their objectives through political connections in London and had turned to building bases of support in the colonies.

There were two such groups of men. One included those colonial assemblymen who had previously sought the influence of British political factions in obtaining provincial patronage. The transatlantic cooperation between English and American factions had been deteriorating since 1715, but the late 1740's and early 1750's saw what was clearly the last attempt at association between such groups. In these years one set of colonial factions, which included all the expansionists that Egnal has studied (proprietary leaders in Pennsylvania and Maryland, the anti-DeLancey party in New York, and Governor Shirley's friends in Massachusetts), sought help from a wing of the English Whigs led by the Duke of Bedford, who was himself an advocate of an aggressive policy against the French, while their opponents had connections with the Duke of Newcastle's more pacifistic wing of the ministry. By the late 1750's, however, the lines of association had become confused, and it was clear that these last attempts at transatlantic factional alliances had proved abortive. At the same time, increasing numbers of Englishmen were being appointed to colonial positions, and it seemed that the only way for aspiring colonists to win political office was to control those appointments from the colonies. In such circumstances, provincial politicians simply found it more worthwhile to develop a sound base of support in the colonies, where they might wring concessions from the governors, than to continue their efforts to cultivate connections in England.

The other set of men who became similarly convinced of the futility of looking to London for political help included the leaders of a number of different colonial interest groups. Several types of interest groups had relied on their English supporters in the first half of the eighteenth century—among them religious organizatons, mercantile associations, and non-English immigrant societies. Churches and mercantile groups had enjoyed the help of their English counterparts, who lobbied before the Board of Trade and Privy Council for the allowance or disallowance of local laws or the interpretation of English policies in their favor. Immigrant communities had similar support from a variety of English sources—the merchants who shipped them over, the churches that provided ministers, and the philanthropists who raised funds for them. But by the mid-eighteenth century the interest group connections, like the factional alliances, were weakening. The Great Awakening drove a wedge between the revitalized American churches and the complacent English ones which failed completely to see what the provincials were getting excited about. The escalating controversies over colonial paper money, among other things, created a rift between English and American merchants. Questions about the assimilability of foreigners and the administration of funds sent to assist them seem to have curtailed English aid to immigrant groups. Whatever the reasons, and they varied, English lobbyists provided markedly less help for American interests after 1750. Thus colonial interest groups, like the factions, ceased to depend on English protection and stressed the development of provincial support.

The issue of expansion happened to be of particular interest both to politicians who had lost their English connections and to interest groups that had lost their English lobbies. Politicians in the proprietary, anti-DeLancey, and Shirley parties felt betrayed by their former expansionist allies in England. Land companies and groups of non-English settlers felt expansion to be vital to their interests. Churches divided for and against expansion, depending on their evangelical, frontier orientation. Even merchant groups divided, depending on whether or not they regarded western lands as an opportunity for investment. Thus, in the 1740's and after, colonial politics was characterized by the emergence of a province-oriented leadership concerned to develop a power base in the colonies and interested enough in expansion to make that a major issue.[11]

Locally, the issue of expansion provided an effective focus for political organization among lesser assemblymen and interested constituents—and this seems to have been true whether one favored or opposed the expansionist view. Moreover, expansion was an issue on which a great variety of local interest groups could develop a partisan orientation. Some church groups supported the Protestant, missionary side of expansion, but on the other hand, as Egnal shows, Quaker pacifism in Pennsylvania and Anglican concern in New York about the maintenance of stability and hierarchy made these groups anti-expansionist. Frontiersmen, land speculators, and established town dwellers considering a move to the frontier were all concerned with the relationship between expansion and land values; immigrant groups were interested in obtaining fertile land on which to settle. Expansion—or containment—therefore provided an issue around which far-ranging coalitions could form.

Another aspect of the expansionist issue is that it encouraged people in small villages, whose political horizons had never extended much beyond the town meeting or county court, to become interested in politics at the provincial level. There is a good deal of evidence that colonists outside of capital cities had not shown substantial interest in assembly politics from 1715 to 1750. But such issues as defense, Indian relations, and paper money affected everyone, and the rapid rise in their importance at mid-century prompted many colonists to take an interest in what their assemblies were doing. They were thus susceptible to party appeals as they had not been before.

Within the assemblies, questions relating to defense, Indian relations, and paper money appear to have increased more rapidly than did proprietary, urban–rural, or ecclesiastical issues. The number of laws relating to defense and Indian relations, for example, jumped from one in all the colonies between 1730 and 1735 to thirty-seven between 1760 and 1765. By consistently voting together on such issues, colonial assemblymen may have acquired habits of cooperation that lasted beyond specific issues. If one accepts the arguments of Maurice Duverger that in modern parliamentary democracies political parties commonly emerged from the increasingly consistent grouping together of representatives, then expansion would be a likely issue around which such parties might begin.[12]

But if expansionism appears to have been effective in creating political groupings at the local and provincial level, and in arousing pro- and anti-British sentiments, can we say it was the *most* significant issue, as Egnal seems to suggest? A number of other contemporary problems might be considered as alternative or complementary sources of party division, such as, for example, the challenges directed toward proprietary governments, east–west sectionalism, or any number of religious issues. The question is simply which set of alignments provides the broadest and most consistent division in pre-Revolutionary politics. To find out, we will have to study such meager voting records as exist, determine which issue developed the most consistent alignments among the assemblymen, and then determine which alignments carried over to the greatest number of other issues. All this is simply to say that the best explanation is the one that explains the most.

We also need to know which type of division provides the best explanation for the way in which popular partisanship was mobilized. Proprietary supporters, churchgoers, town dwellers, rural politicians clustered around the county courts would all have had "built-in centers of support"—that is, they could develop their partisan appeals from previously established institutions. But expansionists and anti-expansionists could not; except for the land companies, they had few pre-established institutions directly committed to their point of view. This may actually have been an advantage, forcing them to create political followings that transcended existing ones and giving them flexibility in appealing to uncommitted voters, but we cannot be sure until this aspect of the problem has been studied.

Once having found the issue which most fully explains alignments both within and without the assemblies, we need to ask further whether the same issue also serves best to identify Whigs and Tories in the Revolution. That proprietary and anti-proprietary positions toward the Revolution were reversed in Maryland and Pennsylvania, and that in Virginia both the "proprietor" Lord Fairfax and his local opponents went into the Revolution with equal enthusiasm, suggest that the proprietary issue is not a good one for explaining Revolutionary divisions. But other divisive issues remain. There is at least a strong possibility that members of religious minorities in every colony were far more inclined to be Loyalist than were their local majorities. We are only beginning to look at the question of urban versus rural origins of the Revolution, but Stephen Patterson's study of Massachusetts suggests that small towns tended to be far more hostile to the British than were their more cosmopolitan urban rivals. And there are other problems in using the expansion issue to explain Whig–Tory differences. One can explain away the Tory sympathies of well-known expansionists like Daniel Dulaney by counting them as exceptions, but how can we account for the Tory sympathies of whole sections of frontiersmen, the very people who, according to Egnal's thesis, should have been the most fervent of Whigs? And when Egnal says that during the Revolution "Party lines. . . enabl[ed] leaders in one colony to share the perspectives of those in another—an essential precondition for Revolutionary cooperation," it is well to ask whether the "shared perspectives" did not amount to competing desires for the same land and, hence, impediments to cooperation, or at least to Whig cooperation?

In short, only by comparing expansionism with other issues can we say which—if indeed any single issue or cluster of issues—provides the best explanation for Revolutionary attitudes. If expansionism does prove to be the issue most capable of explaining partisan divisions in mid-eighteenth-century America, and if the expansionists and their opponents turn out to coincide reasonably well with Patriots and Loyalists, then Egnal's argument may open the way to a new understanding of the Revolutionary period.

"Greedy Party Work":
The South Carolina Election of 1768

David R. Chesnutt

Thousands of backcountry Regulators flooded into the South Carolina lowcountry to demand the right to vote in the assembly election of 1768, while in the hub of the province hundreds of mechanics pushed for the election of a strong Whig slate to represent the two Charleston parishes. The Regulators saw the election as a means of achieving broad political and social reforms. The mechanics saw it as a means of forcing the Commons House to take a vigorous stand against the Townshend duties. Neither group sustained its political unity beyond the next election, in 1769, yet both threatened briefly to alter the structure of politics in South Carolina. Both movements were stigmatized as so much "greedy party work,"[1] a contemporary evaluation that reflected a typical eighteenth-century abhorrence of political combinations and failed to recognize that each group had well-defined goals which formed the basis of its commitment to specific candidates in the 1768 election.

Elite dominance and the absence of faction and party have long been recognized as the most distinctive traits of pre-Revolutionary politics in South Carolina. Jack P. Greene and Eugene M. Sirmans have carefully delineated the emerging dominance of the gentry-led Commons House, and Robert M. Weir has offered a lucid and comprehensive explanation of the growth of an elite consensus which accompanied the gentry's rise to power between 1735 and 1765. The elimination of divisive economic conflicts between merchants and planters in the early 1730's coupled with the gradual emergence of a unified, prosperous plantation economy diminished special-interest alignments. Marriages among the families of merchants, planters, and lawyers blurred distinctions, as did the blending of agricultural and commercial spheres. Merchants became planters and planters merchants. Thus the gentry managed to achieve a level of prosperity unique in the southern colonies without political infighting over land, commercial advantage, or the Indian trade. Although good planting land had become scarce by the 1750's, the lateral expansion of the rice and indigo cultures into Georgia in that decade and into East Florida in the 1760's alleviated another potential source of internal dissention. Moreover, a mounting anxiety about slavery also promoted cohesiveness among whites as they witnessed the continued growth of a black majority in the provinicial population.

The colony's political structure also worked against faction and party, for by the early 1760's the Commons House had eclipsed the royal establishment headed by the colonial governor. As early as 1744, Governor James Glen had declared with chagrin that the province's frame of government was "unhinged." The absence of lucrative patronage stripped Glen and his successors of a major source of political power and eliminated one of the most common causes of factionalism. Four years later Glen lodged a further complaint about the low ebb of his office: "much of the executive part of the Government and of the Administration, is by various Laws lodged in different setts of Commissioners. Thus we have commissioners of the Market, of the Work house, of the Pilots, of Fortifications and so on, without number." Indeed, when the Commons House chose to do so, it could paralyze the workings of government in order to wring concessions from the royal governors. In the Gadsden Election controversy the House resolved to do no public business with Governor Thomas Boone until he apologized for barring Christopher Gadsden from his seat in the previous assembly. In spite of the pressing demand for a response to the Creek Indian outrages in this period, the House refused to act from December 1762 until after Boone left the province in May 1764. A similar deadlock immobilized provincial affairs during the Wilkes Fund controversy between 1769 and 1775. In both instances the British ministry tacitly recognized the inability of its governors to cope with the powerful Commons House by replacing them.

Finally, the widespread acceptance of Bolingbroke's "country ideology" contributed to the emergence of an ideological consensus which served to unify the upper classes even further. This philosophy, which denigrated party and faction while venerating independence and "the common good," justified for many South Carolinians the summary dismissal of political activity by the Regulators and the mechanics as "greedy party work."[2] Despite all these inhibiting elements, however, both the Regulators and the mechanics emerged as forces to be reckoned with in the election of 1768.

The Regulators posed a direct threat to the political hegemony of the lowcountry elite. They had first appeared in the summer and fall of 1767, as the emergent gentry of the backcountry organized a force to expel marauding bands of outlaws. Soon the vigilante movement broadened its scope to encompass social and political reforms which reflected the aspirations of a large proportion of the backcountry.[3] The key issue which pushed the Regulators into a confrontation with the lowcountry was the Circuit Court Act of 1768. The law met Regulator demands for the establishment of courts, sheriffs, and judicial reforms relating to fees and procedures, but the assembly's inclusion of a clause granting "good behaviour" tenure to judges made it likely that the bill would be disallowed in London. Crown-appointed judges traditionally served "at pleasure" in order to tie them to the royal establishment. The legislators' futile attempts to remove Chief Justice Charles Shinner in 1767 on grounds of incompetence formed the background of their decision to write the good behavior proviso into the new law. Acknowledging that the tenure issue might bring disallowance, the assembly instructed its colonial agent Charles Garth to use his utmost influence to gain acceptance for the law in London.[4] Regulator leaders felt, however, that the assembly had sacrificed their local interests for an abstract principle and responded by adopting a plan to take the backcountry out of the jurisdiction of the Charleston courts. Under this "General Plan of Regulation" the Regulators decreed that no writ from the Charleston courts could be served without their prior consent. This move secured their leaders from being arrested and jailed at Charleston and generated additional pressure for the creation of circuit courts. Their plan worked well, successfully withstanding even the direct challenge of the Provost Marshal Roger Pinckney. When Pinckney marched into the backcountry to arrest a Regulator for interfering with his process servers, the Regulators defied him and forced him to return to the capital empty-handed. Nor were the efforts of Lieutenant Governor William Bull more effective. Bull sought to restore authority over the backcountry by offering a general amnesty to the Regulators, and as a gesture of his good will pardoned a Regulator convicted of burning down the home of a man suspected of aiding the outlaw bands which plundered the backcountry. Bull's efforts met with silence among the Regulators.[5]

Encouraged by their success in blocking legal process, the Regulators shifted their attention in the fall of 1768 to the approaching assembly election. Only three parishes had been established in the backcountry, and each had but one seat in the assembly. Under the leadership of Tacitus Gaillard, however, the Regulators devised a plan to gain a more proportional representation in the Commons House. The lowcountry parishes south of the Santee River were laid out roughly in the shape of rectangles, with the short side of the rectangle running either along the coast or parallel to it, and the long sides running inland perpendicular to the coast. Arguing that the parishes were still open on the interior side, Gaillard and his followers extended the side boundaries of parishes like St. James Goosecreek, St. Bartholomew, and St. Paul deep into the backcountry. The *Gazette* reported in August that the Regulators had been "at great trouble" to determine the parish lines, and in a private letter Peter Timothy explained that the Regulators intended "to regulate our ensuing Election by marching down 100 or 150 men to every Parish where they have a Right . . . to vote."[6]

To give added weight to the new representatives they expected to elect, the Regulators made concurrent plans for a mass march on Charleston. A letter from Camden not only gave the details of the planned march but tried to assuage the lowcountry's fear of violence.

The Regulators were to meet in Camden on October 5 to draw up a list of grievances for presentation to the assembly. Then, on October 10, some 2,500 to 3,000 men were to meet at Eutaw for the march in order "to pursue the proper Measures for Redress." Regulators from the Congarees, Broad, and Saluda rivers were not to march, but were to hold themselves in readiness "in case they should be wanted." The letter closed by declaring that the marchers did not intend "the least injury to any Person in Town, desiring only provisions and quarters untill their Complaints shall be heard." Several weeks later Timothy's *Gazette* put forth a more alarming report that the Regulators intended "not only to have their Grievances *heard* but also *redressed,* so far as it may appear to be in the *power* of the legislature."[7]

In spite of fears in the lowcountry that "great disorder" would reign in the country parishes, the election proceeded quietly. The Regulators "behaved every where with decency and propriety" as they came down to cast their votes. In the backcountry parishes they elected William Thompson for St. Matthew, Benjamin Farrar for St. Mark, and Claudius Pegues for St. David. In the lowcountry the Regulators successfully dominated the polls at St. James Goosecreek, electing three of their own, Tacitus Gaillard, Aaron Loocock, and Moses Kirkland.[8] Gaillard was also returned for St. George Dorchester, which seems to indicate some Regulator activity there. Gaillard's brother Theodore and Regulator sympathizer Charles Canty were returned for Prince Frederick. The Regulators also came down to St. Paul and St. Bartholomew. They were allowed to vote in St. Paul, but the parish returned three lowcountry planters. In St. Bartholomew the churchwardens refused to allow them to cast their ballots. In the final analysis, the Regulators could claim the election of six men and possibly the victories of three other candidates. They lost the three contested seats in St. Paul and were blocked in their bid for the four seats of St. Bartholomew.[9] Thus it seemed the new assembly was to be faced with a bloc of members committed to redress the grievances of the backcountry. How successful they might have been was never tested, however, because the assembly's endorsement of the Massachusetts Circular Letter opposing the Townshend Acts led to the dissolution of the Commons House before most backcountry members could take their seats.

The Charleston mechanics did not become an organized force in the 1768 election until three days before the polling began. Their rally opened with a barbecue and speeches against the Townshend duties, followed by the selection of candidates for both Charleston parishes. They closed the day's proceedings by formally dedicating the city's "Liberty Tree":[10]

> About 5 o'clock, they all removed to a most noble LIVE-OAK Tree, in Mr. Mazyck's pasture, which they formally dedicated to LIBERTY, where many loyal, patriotic, and constitutional toasts were drank, beginning with *the glorious NINETY-TWO Anti-Rescinders of Massachusetts-Bay,* and ending with, *Unanimity among the Members of our ensuing Assembly not to rescind from the said Resolutions,* each succeeded by three huzzas.

South Carolina seemed to be marking time as Massachusetts and Virginia stepped forth boldly against the duties. All three Charleston newspapers had given full coverage to the controversy in Massachusetts. The Massachusetts Circular Letter of February 1768, calling for a united statement of principle against the acts, did not reach Charleston until after the previous Commons House had adjourned. Responding for the Carolina assembly, House Speaker Peter Manigault pointed out that the colony's provincial agent had been instructed to work with other agents to obtain repeal of the duties.[11] When Governor Francis Bernard called the Massachusetts General Court into session and demanded rescission of the circular letter, the legislators refused by a majority of 92 to 17. Bernard then dissolved the legislature as instructed by Lord Hillsborough in his circular letter to the American governors.[12]

When the merchants of Boston appealed to their Charleston counterparts to unite with them in a non-importation movement in the fall of 1768, they met with silence.[13] Money was tight and the Charleston merchants did not need the disruption of non-importation to compound their problems. Indeed, the merchants were looking forward to a reopening of the slave trade in January to ease the money problem. In the years before the ban the planters' investments in slaves had offset the sale of their crops, and the Charleston merchants had been able to maintain a fairly liquid position. After the prohibitive duties on slaves took effect in January 1766, the planters began to accumulate surplus capital. By the fall of 1768 the planters were in the driver's seat, able to demand cash or discounted bills for their crops.[14] Regulator activities in the summer and fall of 1768 also put a damp on the question of responding to the Townshend duties.[15]

The slate of candidates endorsed by the mechanics for the two Charleston parishes included Christopher Gadsden, Benjamin Dart, Thomas Smith of Broad Street, Thomas Smith, Sr., Thomas Savage, and Hopkin Price. All were from the city's upper class. Three candidates had impeccable credentials as members of the first rank: Christopher Gadsden, a successful factor with extensive landholdings; Benjamin Dart, a prosperous merchant whose family ranked among the leading planters; and Thomas Smith of Broad Street, a wealthy merchant-planter whose fortune had been built on the slave trade. The other candidates were men of lesser prestige and wealth but clearly from the upper levels of society. Thomas Smith, Sr. was an elderly retailing merchant; Thomas Savage was a rising young merchant from a good family; Hopkin Price was a successful mechanic who had moved into the upper class. A tanner, Price had acquired property and tenements in Charleston as well as a small plantation on the Ashley River. Price's first election to the Commons House by St. Helena's parish in 1760 signified his move into a higher circle, but that his acceptance was far from automatic was reflected in Henry Laurens' scornful comment on Price's re-election in 1762: "I don't know any public affair worth communicating but the election of Mr. Hopkin Price to a Legislative chair in the Stadt House as one of the representatives of the oppulent & discerning people of Charles Town." This was the only election after 1757 in which Laurens was not chosen as a member from Charleston. Although Price served almost five years in the Commons House, he never achieved a position of leadership during his legislative career.[16] Nevertheless, Price would have been the one candidate with whom the mechanics could most closely identify. According to a newspaper account of the rally, the six candidates had been chosen by a "great majority" of the mechanics. Yet there were four other men who had also been considered by the mechanics.

The four men passed over by the mechanics were Henry Laurens, Charles Pinckney, John Lloyd, and John Ward. The *Gazette* reported that "great diligence is used in canvassing and interest making, by the friends of the different candidates, as well by others as by the Mechanicks.—particularly in favor of Mr. Price, Mr. Laurens, Mr. Pinckney, Mr. Lloyd, Mr. Savage, and Mr. Ward."[17] There was little difference between the four men passed over by the mechanics and the six nominated by them. Henry Laurens, a prominent merchant-planter, and Charles Pinckney, a leading lawyer, were men of the first rank. Both had long careers in the Commons House and were leading members in almost every session. John Lloyd and John Ward were lesser merchants, both relatively young men, and both without experience in the Commons House.[18] The only characteristic which distinguishes these four men from the six nominated was the mechanics' belief that the six would be more zealous in opposing the Townshend duties.

The character of the candidates under consideration reveals much about the political attitudes of the mechanics' party as a whole. In agreeing to support candidates from the upper class, the mechanics acquiesced to the old order of politics in South Carolina. Their slate did not challenge the hegemony of the lowcountry elite. The mechanics had simply expressed a preference for one segment of the elite—a segment of "gentry Whigs"— as opposed to another. Those gentry Whigs, apparently aware that support for their candidates would be forthcoming, had provided the impetus for the initial organization of the mechanics which came during the election rally. The *Gazette* noted that the "entertainment" of the day had been furnished by some of the men subsequently nominated by the mechanics. In a private letter Henry Laurens described the affair as a "Grand Barbacu given by a very Grand Simpleton."[19] Although neither source identified the organizers by name, Christopher Gadsden's leadership of the mechanics during the Stamp Act crisis, his caustic relations with Laurens, and his subsequent leadership in bringing about non-importation make him the logical choice as principal organizer.

In the election of 1768 the mechanics could claim only moderate success. Half of their slate, Gadsden, Dart, and Savage, won seats in the new assembly. The other three seats went to Laurens, Pinckney, and Lloyd. The defeat of Hopkin Price is worth comment. Price lost by six votes, a defeat which came directly at the hands of Laurens, who gave up twenty of his own votes to put Pinckney in over Price.[20] Though the mechanics' candidates had won only three seats, the ensuing assembly brought a complete victory—a unanimous vote to support the Massachusetts Circular Letter. What they failed to win at the polls the mechanics won in the assembly itself.

While elite leadership in no way diminished the political effectiveness of the mechanics in the 1768 election, it does help to explain why the mechanics did not continue as a viable force in subsequent assembly elections before the Revolution. As later events revealed, the political activities of the mechanics always moved in concert with those of the gentry Whigs because the mechanics were neither well enough organized nor sufficiently confident to chart an independent course.[21] They became an adjunct of the gentry Whigs, and when the gentry chose not to mobilize them in subsequent elections, the ephemeral character of their politics became fully apparent.

The electioneering in Charleston succeeded in raising a popular clamor for a vigorous response to the Townshend duties. In mid-October Lieutenant Governor Bull observed: "There are many here who entertain favorable sentiments of . . . the political principles now prevailing in Boston, which kindles a kind of enthusiasm very apt to predominate in popular Assemblies and whose loud cries silence the weaker Voice of Moderation." Bull informed Hillsborough that he had prorogued the assembly and that he hoped the delay would "give time to many who have suffered themselves hitherto to be carried away in the stream of popular opinion to examine things cooly."[22]

When the assembly finally convened on November 15, Bull's hopes seemed justified. Though the members of the Commons House assembled with unusual promptness, Henry Laurens did not perceive a sense of urgency within the House. In the early morning hours before the assembly convened for its third day, Laurens commented: "Our House of Assembly is to present their Speaker this morning, but according to my ideas, we shall enter upon no business before the Holy Days."[23] Laurens' own moderation apparently blunted his perception. The proceedings of the House would be sufficiently defiant to bring dissolution within two days.

What provoked the Commons into action? The House journals are silent on this point, but they do provide clues to the mood of the membership. Twenty-two members had assembled on the opening day of the session, which fell on a Tuesday, November 15. This was an unusually high turnout; the assembly seldom achieved a quorum until a week or so after being called together. All of the men present that first day were either from Charleston or neighboring lowcountry parishes. By the end of the week a total of twenty-six members would qualify. Only one representative of the backcountry, Tacitus Gaillard, would be included in that number. Although the members chose their Speaker on the opening day, the formal organization could not be completed until Thursday morning, when the House presented the Speaker and received the governor's opening address. Governor Charles Montagu urged the assembly to enact new laws to regulate the Indian trade, to garrison Fort Charlotte and Fort Prince George, and to pass laws which would relieve "the distresses of your fellow subjects in the remote parts of this province, and at the same time discourage, and if possible, entirely prevent, for the future, such illegal insurrections as have for some months past appeared in those parts." Sandwiched between these requests was the admonition "to discountenance and treat with the contempt it deserves, any letter or paper that may appear to have the smallest tendency to sedition, or by promoting unwarrantable combination, to inflame the minds of the people, to oppose the authority of parliament, or the government of our Gracious Sovereign." Montagu thus called attention to the two issues uppermost in the minds of the House members—the backcountry, and the Townshend duties. Immediately after Montagu's speech, William Wragg and John Freer informed the House that they would not serve. Later that same day three other men declined to serve, Rawlins Lowndes, Peter Sinkler, and Daniel Heyward. And the following morning, Joseph Allston also declined.[24] The refusals by royalist William Wragg and by Rawlins Lowndes are important indications that the Commons House was moving toward a confrontation with Montagu over the Townshend duties.

Wragg and Lowndes held different political views, yet both probably declined for the same reason: to disassociate themselves from a potentially disloyal assembly. Wragg had long been one of the Crown's most vocal supporters in South Carolina. When the assembly had moved to erect a statue of William Pitt in 1766, Wragg had countered with a proposal to erect a statute of the king. When the Whig John Mackenzie had called for the re-electon of only those men who stood firmly behind American resistance, Wragg reaffirmed his position publicly and suggested that his constituents elect someone else. When Wragg was then elected, he hailed it as a vindication of his royalist position. Here was a staunch king's friend.[25] Rawlins Lowndes' attitude was more ambiguous. As an assistant judge of the court of common pleas, he had tried to reopen the court without stamped paper in defiance of Chief Justice Charles Shinner. Lowndes' politics are perhaps best explained by Lieutenant Governor Bull, who later noted that Lowndes refused to subscribe to non-importation "as being incompatible with his office, ... yet he maintains those arguments which deny the supreme legislative authority in the Parliament of Great Britain over the British colonies."[26] Thus while Lowndes' refusal to serve appears to have been a move to extricate himself from a situation that might call for a public stand against imperial taxaion, Wragg's critics would later accuse him of currying favor with the imperial authorities.[27]

As though to offset the refusals to serve, Thomas Lynch, the leading Whig among the planters, appeared at the door of the assembly early the next day to take his seat. Lynch was the twenty-sixth and last member to qualify. The House made its decision to deal with the Townshend duties the same morning by requesting that the

Speaker read the circular letters opposing them from Massachusetts and Virginia. The letters were then referred to a committee dominated by the Charleston members and headed by James Parsons. Parsons made the "unanimous" report of his committee when the House reassembled Saturday morning, placing before it a series of resolutions endorsing the letters. These resolutions were in turn approved by the "unanimous" vote of the twenty-six members of the Commons House. Reading the House journal that evening, Governor Montagu promptly dissolved the assembly "by beat of drum." When the *Gazette* concluded its report of the assembly's proceedings the next week, it noted that the new toast of the town was "the UNANIMOUS TWENTY-SIX."[28]

The decision of the Commons House to put aside the backcountry problems and deal with the question of imperial taxation was not entirely surprising. In the Circuit Court Act of 1768 the assembly had shown that it considered an imperial issue more important than one of only local interest. And while the House had shown some sympathy toward the grievances of the Regulators, its members were clearly distressed by the westerners' unruly behavior. The Regulators' violent methods in dealing with outlaws, the abrasive and abusive language of their petitions to the House, their refusal to allow writs to be served, their failure to obey the orders of the provost marshal, and their threats of a mass march on Charleston to force a redress of grievances were all outside the acceptable limits of behavior in the lowcountry. When the assembly met in mid-November rumors of the march had diminished, but the Regulators remained an unpredictable and potentially disruptive element in South Carolina politics.

No doubt some of the legislators shared the views of William Bull, who believed that members of the Commons House elected by Regulator votes might serve as a check on the lowcountry Whigs who were pressing for action against the Townshend duties. Unanimity had become a byword in the lowcountry, the key to showing the imperial authorities the solidarity of the population and the depth of South Carolina's resentment over the new taxes. And there may have been a desire by some of the members to show the rest of the colonies that South Carolinians were even more dedicated to the preservation of liberty than the citizens of Massachusetts, whose representatives had divided on the question of rescission.[29] But could the assembly present a united front if the backcountry leaders joined in the deliberations of the House? Would the Regulator leaders forego local interests for the sake of standing united against the imperial menace? Or would they call down the marchers if the assembly refused to come to terms with their demands? Faced with these questions, the assembly sidestepped the backcountry issues by the simple expedient of bringing up the Townshend duties before most of the backcountry representatives had arrived in Charleston. Tacitus Gaillard, the only Regulator leader then present, was as much a lowcountry planter as he was a spokesman of the backcountry. The rapid adoption of the resolutions supporting Massachusetts and the immediate dissolution of the assembly by Governor Montagu were accomplished before the other backcountrymen could take their seats. The appearance of unanimity was thus preserved, and blame for the postponement of backcountry problems could be assigned to the governor himself.

Circumstances altered swiftly in the interval between the dissolution of the Commons House in November and the convening of a new House in June 1769. A court order to arrest six Regulators, placed in the hands of a "notorious Rogue," one Joseph Coffel, provided an excuse to raise a counterforce of backcountry "Moderators." The Moderators included a number of outlaws who had been targets of the Regulators. As Coffel and his men moved into the backcountry they "appropriated" provisions at will, placing families in fear for both their lives and property. Many of the backcountrymen were already on their way down to the lowcountry to vote in the new assembly election of March 1769 when they learned of Coffel's depredations. They quickly turned back, organized a force to oppose Coffel, and confronted the Moderators on the banks of the Saluda River. There both sides agreed to disband. Assessing the impact of the Moderators on the outcome of the 1769 election, Charles Woodmason interpreted the whole affair as part of a plot to keep backcountry members out of the assembly. Woodmason ignored the Regulators' success in electing five of their candidates in five parishes and in casting their ballots in two other parishes. The second important development during the legislative interim was the gentry Whigs' decision to change the forum of resistance against the Townshend duties from the Commons House to the Charleston newspapers. The assembly thus achieved a brief respite from imperial questions, and this in turn paved the way for a consideration of the backcountry demands.[30]

The new assembly which met in June seemed ready to come to terms with the backcountry. The Commons House quickly revised the disallowed Circuit Court Act of 1768 to meet the objections raised by the Board of Trade, eliminating the "good behaviour" tenure clause, placing the appointments of sheriffs under the governor, and providing permanent salaries for the judges, attorney general, and clerk of the court. In selecting commissioners to supervise construction of courthouses and jails, the assembly included the names of seven ex-Regulators.[31] The assembly made another important concession in its decision to allow backcountry participation in elections in the open parishes of the lowcountry. Voters living at a distance were required only to produce a certificate which identified them as freeholders in the parish where they claimed voting privileges.[32]

The concessions of 1769 answered the major concerns of the Regulator leaders. They now had a fabric of law to protect their property as well as assurances of somewhat broader opportunities to participate in the elective process. The concessions also represented a satisfying recognition of their status as community leaders, a status that would be constantly reinforced by their service as grand jurors, commissioners of record, and officers of the court. For now the backcountry gentry seemed content to put aside the social and political reforms inherent in their initial demands for parish reorganization. They withdrew their support from the Regulation, ending their challenge to lowcountry control of the provincial political structure. The accommodation of the rising upcountry gentry ended the Regulator movement as an organized political force. The province was left with only sporadic vigilante actions and an occasional grand jury presentment to remind them of the backcountry's short-lived challenge to the old order.

The concessions of 1769 signified an assimilation of the backcountry gentry into the political establishment of the province. Post-election developments among the mechanics brought a similar absorption of their leaders. The inclusion of the mechanics, however, took place outside the normal political channels in a new political substructure which emerged in the summer of 1769.

The mechanics had first risen to power in the Stamp Act crisis of 1765, but much of their new-found status was eroded following the repeal of the act in the spring of 1766. They "sunk into nothing," in the words of former House Speaker Benjamin Smith. The gathering of the "Liberty Boys" in the fall of 1766 indicated just how low they had fallen. Less than thirty mechanics and only one of the gentry Whigs from Charleston, Christopher Gadsden, attended. Their pledge to "Liberty" after Gadsden's harangue against the Declaratory Act did not even receive notice in the local newspapers.[33]

Not until the "Grand Barbacu" in 1768 did the mechanics regain center stage. That rally revealed the gentry Whigs' determination to renew the strategy which had been so effective against the Stamp Act: a formal protest from the assembly supported by the threat of mob action "out of doors." With the adoption of the "unanimous resolves" against the Townshend Acts by a bare quorum of the assembly, the Whigs secured the first part of their plan. Next came the move to establish non-importation, but this time the Whigs devised a more formal pattern of resistance to supplant the mobs which had proved somewhat difficult to control in the Stamp Act crisis. Gadsden, Thomas Lynch, and John MacKenzie furnished the impetus for the non-importation scheme. With support from the mechanics and the lowcountry planters, they were able to force the merchants into a general non-importation association on July 22, 1769. The final step which formalized resistance was the creation of the Committee of Thirty-nine to police the association. The committee—composed of thirteen mechanics, thirteen planters, and thirteen merchants—served as a vehicle for reconciling class interests.[34]

The political substructure created in 1769 and enlarged in the successive crises of the pre-Revolutionary era served the gentry Whigs well. The prestige and visibility which the mechanic leaders gained from the Charleston committees eliminated the necessity of continuing their involvement in assembly politics. Moreover, their inclusion in the machinery of resistance gave the Whigs an excuse to prod their more conservative brethren, and at the same time checked any possible mechanic excesses which might damage the cause of liberty. Abandoning their "party" tactics of 1768, the gentry Whigs returned to their old custom of settling differences with their fellow gentry behind the closed doors of the assembly, re-establishing once again the facade of elite solidarity in the face of imperial antagonism.

Neither upcountry threats nor urban mobilization significantly changed the power structure of colonial South Carolina. The "greedy party work," so demeaningly described by William Drayton, was the merest rent in the curtain which usually hid the wires controlling South Carolina's political machinery. After 1769 the political magic show would continue with the drapery firmly in place.

Factionalism of the sort that could mobilize New York and Boston mechanics or Pennsylvania backwoodsmen never gained ground in South Carolina. The political divisions among the elite that might have encouraged contending parties to politicize the mob never opened. Part of the explanation for South Carolina's political stability lay in the cohesiveness of the gentry: their commonly held ideology, the ties of kinship, the homogeneity of the economic structure, and the adversary role taken up by the assembly in opposition to the royal establishment. But other, more factious colonies also shared common ideologies, intermarried elites, and other characteristics similar to those which bound together the Carolina gentry. What then made South Carolina different?

Contending parties usually contest for power and control of scarce resources. In New York, Massachusetts, and Pennsylvania the contention was for land, Indian contracts, and patronage, and the usual route to the political preference that brought such rewards was through the provincial administration. In South Carolina the royal governors exercised nominal control over land, but there was little significance in this by the 1760's. Good planting lands had long since been taken up in South Carolina, and those who sought new land tended to look to Georgia and East Florida where it could be had for the asking. The provincial Indian trade had been controlled by the Commons House almost without interruption from 1707 until 1765 through a series of agents, commissioners, and directors appointed by the House. By the mid-1760's the Commons was willing to relinquish its control only because the Indian trade no longer figured as an important avenue of wealth for the lowcountry gentry. As for patronage, the Commons House took care to retain control of the officers paid from provincial funds, and legislative commissions directed the expenditures for public works of all kinds. In short, South Carolina's royal governors had few gifts to bestow upon their adherents. Even the governors' recommendations for high office were of little value in building a political base of loyal supporters, as few members of the provincial gentry were willing to accept a seat on the council or an appointment to the court.

South Carolina's brush with factional politics in 1768 reflected a determined and continued commitment among the lowcountry gentry to the principle of accommodation, and it testified to the cohesiveness and resiliency of the coterie of merchants, planters, and professional men who formed the upper tier of society. Cohesion did not preclude disagreement, of course; the mobilization of the mechanics revealed the sharp edge of disagreement in 1768. It should be noted, however, that the gentry Whigs did not again resort to the tactics of 1768 to influence the makeup of the assembly. Equally significant was the elite's success in staving off the threat of sectional division. In the wake of the election of 1768, the gentry made room for the aspirations of both lowcountry and upcountry leaders. Moreover, by agreeing to internal reforms, however limited, and encouraging a unified resistance, the assembly reasserted its ability to present a common front in the face of new imperial challenges. By the end of 1769 all sides had been placated, stability had been restored to assembly politics, and the fleeting shadow of "greedy party work" had faded from view.

Another View of the South Carolina Election of 1768 and the Regulators: A Comment

Joseph A. Ernst

This is an interesting story—as far as it goes. Mr. Chesnutt tells us a great deal that we did not know about the South Carolina election of 1768. We learn who was elected, on what issues, and by whom. Chesnutt is especially good at sorting out the "party" divisions over non-importation. His handling of the Regulators is another matter. Because he omits so much of the background and controversy concerning this issue, one can question many of his underlying assumptions about political life in South Carolina and, perhaps, even his views of the place and importance of the 1768 election in the Revolutionary history of the province.

In discussing the Regulators, Chesnutt cites the work of Richard M. Brown and offers the reader three generalizations. One, the Regulators appeared for the first time in the summer and fall of 1767 as a vigilante movement aimed at ridding the backcountry of outlaws. Two, the Regulators came into conflict with the lowcountry elite over the Circuit Court Act of 1768. Because the oligarchy appeared willing to sacrifice backcountry demands for courts by including in the legislation a clause, anathema to authorities in London, for the tenure of judges during "good behaviour," the Regulators adopted a more vigorous opposition to the elite. They blocked the legal process, threatened to march on Charleston, and moved to elect their own representatives. Three, the "determined and continued commitment among the lowcountry gentry to the principle of accommodation" quickly led to the enactment of a new and satisfactory Circuit Court measure in 1769. Thereafter, "the province was left with only sporadic vigilante actions and an occasional grand jury presentment to remind them of the backcountry's short-lived challenge to the old order." All of these assertions require comment and elaboration.[1]

The Regulators did first appear in 1767. Their origin, however, is to be found in the migration into western South Carolina at the end of the French and Indian War. This human tide left in its wake not only great numbers of farmers but also the lawless and the idle. The outlaws inspired several petitions to the assembly in the years 1762-64. But the Commons House, locked in a struggle with Governor Thomas Boone over constitutional rights and privileges arising out of the disputed election of Christopher Gadsden, did nothing.

Failure to respond to backcountry problems threatened to divide the Commons House into factions as early as 1762. These factions anticipated the assembly divisions and conflicts that Chesnutt discovers in 1768. Thus William Wragg, a delegate from St. John Parish and a notorious supporter of the executive and of royal government, in January 1763 wrote an open letter to his constituents in Robert Wells' *South Carolina Weekly Gazette*. Wragg observed that the recent December assembly resolution not to enter into any business with the governor until he had done "justice to this house" meant, among other things, that the public credit would suffer and that money to pay the public bounty to new immigrants and to provide for the safety of the back settlements would not be forthcoming.[2]

Gadsden responded to Wragg's charges, including the assembly's disregard of the public welfare, a month later in an apologia covering eight columns of Peter Timothy's *South Carolina Gazette*. Predictably, Gadsden placed the blame for the impasse on the governor and remarked that if Boone had been a little civil in his dealings with the Commons House, the "whole affair would have [been] dropped." Gadsden's letter elicited a flurry of responses. Most important was a public outburst by Henry Laurens, another of the principals in the political disputes of 1768. Like Wragg, Laurens also seems to have opposed the assembly resolution of December 1762. But in his reply to Gadsden, Laurens focused on the political fault lines that appeared following the Cherokee campaigns of 1760 and 1761 and the altercation between British Colonel James Grant and provincial Colonel Thomas Middleton, a conflict in which Laurens supported Grant and Gadsden Middleton. This newspaper war continued for several months longer.[3]

The Boone affair, meanwhile, wore on through another year. Then, in January 1764, the legislature convened long enough to vote money to suppress the Creek Indians, who were raiding along the frontier, and to qualify new members. By now Boone wanted peace. When two candidates from St. Andrew Parish appeared for the oaths of "abjuration," the governor quietly performed his duty without any mention of his would-be rights to judge their qualifications. Thereupon someone, possibly Wragg or Laurens, moved to dismiss the assembly resolution of December 1762. But the issue had long since become a point of principle, and the compromise motion failed. The members went home, and the House did not reassemble until after Boone quit the province the following spring.[4]

This repeated failure of the Commons House to take up the public business and, particularly, the grievances of the backcountry provoked another outburst from Laurens. The plight of the back settlers was "pitious enough," Laurens observed to a correspondent in February 1764. It cried out for public notice and relief. Laurens went on to denounce a leader in "popular quarrels," obviously Gadsden, who would rather destroy the province than give quarter to the governor. Had Gadsden lived in the backcountry, "or even had £ 1,000 at stake" there, "he would sing a different note."[5]

If the back settlers had few supporters in the assembly, they were not without friends elsewhere in government. One of these friends was Chief Justice Charles Shinner. Chesnutt mentions Shinner only in connection with the "good behaviour" tenure of judges and the Stamp Act. Shinner, however, played a major role in the Regulator affair. Shortly after the Commons House disbanded in late January 1764, the provincial grand jury, under Shinners's instigation, drew official attention to the need for courts in the back settlements, the too-great expense of coming to Charleston for trial, and the need for public schools. The jury reiterated these findings in 1765 and again in 1766.[6]

Another friend of the backcountry was William Bull. He became acting lieutenant governor upon Boone's departure. In January 1765 Bull appealed to the assembly for a system of justice to "suppress in great degree the idlers, and vagabonds who now infest and injure the industrious remote settlers too often with impunity.'"[7] A suitable bill for establishing circuit courts throughout the province came before the House, and on March 28 squeaked through a first reading by a vote of 16 to 15. It failed on second reading.

We do not know why the circuit court bill of 1765 failed. Nothing appears in the assembly journals. But what little we do know concerning the history of courts in colonial South Carolina raises questions about Chesnutt's contention of a "determined and continued commitment among the lowcountry gentry to the principle of accommodation." Thus, two weeks after the failure of the court bill, an anonymous writer offered several observations on the matter to the readers of Timothy's *South-Carolina Gazette*. First, he argued that circuit courts were not impractical but were badly needed to control backcountry violence. Second, he argued against the view that judges and lawyers would be abused by the common people if the courts were located outside of Charleston. "The common people were not hard to manage," he asserted, and were fond of laws. Finally, he argued that self-interest chiefly accounted for the defeat of the circuit courts. The gentry did not oppose the courts as such. But the expense frightened them off. As for the Charleston representatives, that cabal of lawyers and merchants generally opposed the circuit courts because the courts would "in some little measure deprive them of customers."[8]

Such charges had the weight of history behind them. In 1721, shortly after South Carolina became a royal province, "An Act for establishing County Courts and Precinct Courts" outside of Charleston was boycotted by the city lawyers. In 1741 the provincial grand jury resurrected the scheme. The gentry-controlled assembly, however, judged the recommendations "too early" and "too expensive" to put into effect. Another decade passed. Then, in 1752, settlers on the Peedee River petitioned the assembly for a county court. Nothing came of the matter. Another petition from the Peedee, addressed this time to the governor and council, specifically cited as a grievance the distance to the Charleston courts, which deprived the petitioners of the benefits and protection of the laws and exposed the "weak to the oppression of the strong." William Bull, who was lieutenant governor at the time, requested assembly action. But a suitable bill for introducing county courts at Beaufort, Georgetown, and the Congarees in the west never made it past a second reading. Similar petitions and recommendations kept coming in over the next decade—to no avail.[9]

All of these occurrences, it should be noted, took place at the time of the settlement of the so-called middle country of South Carolina, years before the opening of the backcountry. But the assembly had already made its policy clear. There would be no accommodation of new groups; there would be no local government for recently settled areas apart from a limited number of justices of the peace and constables.

This standing policy of refusing to provide the backcountry with any effective local government, coupled with the defeat of the circuit court bill of 1765, elicited from the back settlements a detailed, comprehensive petition for the redress of grievances. When the Commons House reassembled at the beginning of 1766, it received a protest from the inhabitants of Congaree, Ninety-Six, Saluda River, Broad River, and "places adjacent" setting forth at length the troubles and needs of the westerners. Their lands were subject to the same tax rates as the more desirable coastal lands; they needed roads and ferries; they were disenfranchised and unrepresented; they lacked churches and schools; their communities swarmed with outlaws and renegades (white and Indian); and they lacked any court system. Self-interest alone, the petitioners argued, recommended action, since the back people abetted the trade of Charleston and formed a "useful barrier" against Indians and other foes.[10] But as so often before, a relief measure was lost in the House, and the local newspapers carried letter after letter savaging the legislators for scuttling plans for circuit and county courts out of fear both of losing customers at law and in business and of reducing land values in the lowcountry if the backcountry became a more desirable place to live.[11]

If the backcountry settlers and their sympathizers plainly held a conspiracy theory of history, further developments served only to confirm that view.

According to Chesnutt, it was the Circuit Court Act of 1768 which pushed the Regulators into a confrontation with the oligarchy. Specifically, the assembly included in the act a clause granting "good behaviour" tenure to judges who traditionally would have served "at pleasure," a provision that tied them to the royal establishment. This insistence on "good behaviour" tenure, we are told, made it likely that the measure would receive a royal disallowance. But the legislators had felt so frustrated in their efforts to remove Chief Justice Shinner in 1767 on grounds of incompetence that they took the chance and included the controversial clause. The Regulators, in Chesnutt's view, felt that this was too much, that "the assembly had sacrificed their local interests for an abstract principle and responded by adopting" more vigorous plans for opposing the oligarchy. The difficulty with this argument is that it ignores both Shinner's role in the backcountry troubles and the Regulators' views of the attack upon Shinner.

Shinner, as we have seen, had long been a friend of the back settlers. Then, in December 1766, he spent a month in the backcountry in the company of the man who would become the leading Regulator spokesman, the Reverend Charles Woodmason. One of their objectives was to learn firsthand about conditions in the area; another was to help "raise the militia" in a campaign to expel a gang of thieves operating in the Camden area. By this active involvement in the cause of the backcountry, Shinner endeared himself to the people who became Regulators.[12]

While Shinner was out fighting in the west, the Commons House went about organizing an attack of its own. On December 10 the House created a "special committee on the state of the courts of justice" to look into the need to extend the Charleston courts beyond the lowcountry. It might have been expected that the committee's report would have been in the nature of a factual presentation of conditions in the backcountry. The chairman of the committee, however, was Christopher Gadsden, who more than once had opposed accommodating the back settlers. Thus it could not have come as any great surprise that when Gadsden reported to the Commons House early in April 1767, he presented a lengthy indictment of Chief Justice Shinner as a venal and gross character wholly unacquainted with the common law, the acts of the provincial assembly, and the parliamentary statutes. The Commons House recommended Shinner's removal from office, and the governor did receive orders from home to suspend the now dying man. It may be, as Chesnutt argues, that Shinner had become contemptible because of his refusal to open the courts during the Stamp Act crisis. But that was not the whole of it. Shinner had fallen to the malice and revenge of the enemies of the Regulators, wrote Woodmason. "They broke his heart," the minister eulogized. Shinner could truly "be said to have died a martyr for the liberties of the backcountry."[13]

The government's continued failure to defend backcountry rights, property, and lives, and the persecution of the one official who actively involved himself in these matters, finally drove the back settlers to take the offensive against the outlaws in the spring of 1767—rather than for the Regulators to make their first appearance, as Chesnutt puts it.[14] Governor Charles Montagu, who had by this time taken over the reins of government from William Bull, seemed to support the Regulation at first and offered rewards for any bandit leaders brought to Charleston. But when the Regulators talked of coming to the capital in October to "make some complaints," the governor issued a proclamation enjoining "all officers to keep the public peace."[15] He moved closer to open conflict with the Regulators when a month later he asked for legislation "to suppress those licentious spirits" that had "illegally tried, condemned and punished many persons" to the subversion of government and good order.[16]

Before November 1767 it is clear that few members of government either knew or cared much about the backcountry. But on November 7, two days after Montagu's call for suppression of the Regulators, a "Remonstrance" came before the Commons House that summed up in language both angry and eloquent the western resentments of the past five years. The Remonstrance created a furor. Appended to it were twenty-three grievances, major and minor, which the back settlers wanted remedied. The touchstone was the call for "circuit or county courts for the due and speedy administration of justice ... in this as in neighbouring provinces."[17] The first thought was to have the four deputies who had delivered the document jailed and their odious petition burned. But when someone recalled that the four might have been 4,000 demanding redress at the very door of the assembly, cooler heads prevailed. The deputies were feted and "caressed," and as Woodmason, the author of the Remonstrance, later recalled, they left assured that their demands would be "passed into laws."[18]

The Commons House did indeed seem to undertake to placate the back inhabitants. Within days of the reading of the Remonstrance, the House appointed a committee with Wragg as chairman "to consider the state of the province." Twenty-four hours later Wragg, who was already on record as sympathetic to the backcountry, recommended the establishment of circuit *and* county courts, a law for punishing vagrants, and the outfitting for a few months of two companies of soldiers to enforce law and order throughout the back settlements.[19]

In due time a bill came before the House to establish both circuit and county courts. The circuit courts were to enjoy all the powers and jurisdiction of the court of common pleas in Charleston; the county courts were to have jurisdiction in all criminal cases not extending to life and limb and in all civil actions up to £ 20 sterling. But as so often before, a court bill of this kind divided the House and failed to get a third reading. Woodmason claimed that the legislation ran afoul of a "Junto" of lawyers who waited for a "thin house" to rescind the county courts.[20] The measure that appeared during the next assembly session provided for circuit courts only. But as Chesnutt has indicated, this act was compromised by a clause concerning the "good behaviour" tenure of judges that made it likely the legislation would be disallowed at home.

This scuttling of backcountry courts by hostile elements within the assembly late in 1767 and again early in 1768 was doubtless one of the reasons for the adoption in June 1768 of the "General Plan of Regulation," as Chesnutt claims. It was not, however, the only, or even necessarily the most important, reason for the growing animosity between Regulators and government. Immediately after signing the controversial Circuit Court Act in April, and just before leaving the province in May 1768, Governor Montagu ordered the arrest of several Regulator leaders. Their subsequent conviction in the Charleston courts led the Regulators to decree that no further writs from the capital could be served without Regulator consent. In August, a skirmish between the Regulators and the provost marshal, who ignored the decree, ended in the killing of men on both sides. Only the conciliatory policy of Lieutenant Governor William Bull kept matters from getting worse.[21]

Chesnutt's brief discussion of the Regulators' participation in the fall elections of 1768 is excellent. His analysis of the short-lived assembly session in November is also valuable. But his remarks concerning the possible reasons for the assembly's decision to put aside the backcountry problems in favor of the question of imperial taxation are strained. It is probably true that the assembly "considered the imperial issue more important than one of only local interest." But the idea that the House had "shown some sympathy toward the grievances of the Regulators" is hard to accept. So is the apparent effort to shift the responsibility for the assembly decision to the Regulators, who, as Chesnutt puts it, in their "violent methods in dealing with outlaws, the abrasive and abusive language of their petitions to the House, their refusal to allow writs to be served, their failure to obey the orders of the provost marshal, and their threats of a mass march on Charleston to force a redress of grievances were all outside the acceptable limits of behavior in the lowcountry."

Finally, Chesnutt's account of the denouement in the struggle for courts is open to doubt. A court order to arrest six Regulators is said to have "provided an excuse to raise a counterforce of backcountry 'Moderators' " led by Joseph Coffel, a "notorious Rogue." But what we miss here is a subject. It was Montagu who was behind Coffel. After his return to South Carolina in November 1768, Montagu reversed Bull's policy of conciliation. He once more ordered the arrest of Regulator leaders and placed Coffel in charge. The Moderators plundered and harrassed settlers in the Saluda River area for nearly a year and were especially active during the spring elections of 1767, forcing many Regulators to abandon the polls and return home. In their anger the Regulators resolved to march on the lowcountry to "destroy the plantations of those gentlemen" they believed were party to the Coffel appointment and the election raids. Woodmason cooled them down. The Regulators then took a new tack. Despairing of ever receiving redress of their grievances from the lowcountry gentry, "they pitched on the poor parson, and one Mr. *Cary,* a gentleman of the law, to go for England with petitions to his majesty." The mission fizzled when Woodmason refused to leave the province. He considered the mere threat of such an action sufficient to frighten the assembly into placating the Regulators.[22]

Woodmason's assessment of the political situation in 1769 appears to have been correct. During the summer Montagu disavowed the Moderators and Coffel and traveled through the back settlements to patch up a truce. He returned to Charleston with a clutch of petitions and promptly asked for a new circuit court bill meeting all the objections of the ministry. The necessary legislation was passed on July 4, 1769. Montagu sailed for London a few weeks later carrying the court bill with him. He left behind a promise to support the measure all the way to the throne.[23]

The court struggle was not quite over. The day after Montagu signed the Circuit Court Act, a petition arrived requesting the immediate extension of some kind of court system into the backcountry. A special committee called to consider this request recommended to the House that in recognition of the fact that the new circuit court law would not go into effect until the necessary court buildings and jails were erected, a matter of some two years from the time the measure received royal approval, the "Act for establishing County and Precinct Courts" passed back in 1721 be revived as an interim measure. The Commons House rejected the idea.[24] More conciliatory was the course pursued by Bull. With Montagu gone, Bull once more enjoyed a free hand in aiding the back settlements. He pardoned Regulators still under indictment, appointed others to minor posts as militia officers and magistrates, and offered rewards for thieves brought to the Charleston jail.[25]

As Chesnutt notes, the Circuit Court Act of 1769 fulfilled only one, albeit the most important, of the Regulator demands. It did help end "the Regulator movement as an organized political force" as the backcountry leadership withdrew its support from the movement. But it did not, of course, end the rift between backcountry and lowcountry. When the Reverend William Tennent and William Henry Drayton traveled through the back settlements in 1775 to drum up support for the Revolution, they found few friends. The back people, Tennent wrote, had been taught "that no man from Charleston can speak the truth, and that all the papers are full of lies."[26]

One wishes that Chesnutt had traced out the implications of his own important findings about factions and political life in Revolutionary South Carolina. Instead, he seems to be content with the suggestion that his study more or less conforms to the existing paradigms of Richard M. Brown and Robert Weir. But it does not. Brown has argued that there was "no inherent hostility between backcountry and lowcountry;" Weir asserts that the country ideal in South Carolina found expression in a harmony of political leadership and a "disinterested concern" for the welfare of the whole community. Surely, even Chesnutt's tailored discussion of the 1768 election contradicts these views. Yet the fact remains that such matters are never discussed. It is almost as if Chesnutt feels it would be demeaning to discuss such differences in public, as if, to borrow his own metaphor, the investigation of Revolutionary South Carolina must continue with the historiographical "drapery firmly in place."

Parties and the Transformation of the Constitutional Idea in Revolutionary Pennsylvania

George Dargo

Recent scholarship has suggested that in the decade or two before Independence certain conventional, time-honored, Anglo-American notions about the negative effects of party and faction were beginning to change. This was particularly apparent in the middle-colony region, which has aptly been called the "embryo of the new political order."[1] This scholarship does not hold that the accepted wisdom about the evils of party was suddenly abandoned, but rather that it was being subjected to challenges in a number of places for the first time and that these challenges "may not have been quite so ephemeral as we have supposed."[2] The reasons for this reassessment of the role of parties in free government are many, but a major effect of the emergence of factionalism as a fairly regular feature of provincial politics was that it forced those caught up in oppositional groups to attempt to justify their otherwise anomalous position in public life.

Still to be explained, however, is the apparent discontinuity between this first evidence of conceptual change and its disappearance or subsidence, in the Revolutionary and immediate post-Revolutionary period,[3] a particularly surprising decline in view of the important role parties or party-like groups seemed to have played during the Revolution, certainly in Pennsylvania and perhaps elsewhere as well.[4] What I propose in this essay is that the transformation from an unwritten to a written constitutional system — what I call a transition from constitutionalism as process to constitutional formalism — undermined the tentative legitimation that party had achieved with at least some late colonial political activists and thinkers.

To be sure, there were written constitutions of a sort in pre-

98

Revolutionary America — royal and corporate charters, proprietary grants, and other organic instruments — but except for the Massachusetts Charter of 1691 and the 1701 Pennsylvania Charter of Privileges these were little more than grants of power and outlines of procedure. They failed to settle such hotly contested issues as the place of dissenting churches in relation to religious establishments, the role and legitimacy of the press, the real power and authority of the lower houses of assembly, the extent to which common-law rights and liberties were to be enjoyed by colonials, and, most in point, the place of political opposition and oppositional factions in public life.[5] The post-Revolutionary constitutional settlement at the state and federal levels would establish basic ground rules and limits within which public issues were to be debated and resolved, but the drawing up of codes and written instruments of positive law meant that the new constitutional order became frozen in an eighteenth-century mold that could be relieved only partially by the uniquely American institution of judicial review. By contrast, pre-Revolutionary constitutional arrangements were much more open-ended, developmental, and fluid. Positive views of party were possible in the generation before the Revolution precisely because they could be woven into a constantly changing, almost ad hoc, constitutional *process,* whereas in the post-Revolutionary period parties had no place because they were not regarded as part of the legitimate and accepted *form* to which constitutional order had been reduced.

The Revolution did not push American politics in a single, linear, modernist direction, for its effects were contradictory or, at the very least, multifaceted. We do see the emergence of political groupings that at times look modern in function and in some ways even in organization and method.[6] But the Revolution also occasioned attempts to refashion society after older patterns. For some, the American colonies, now independent states, were back in Locke's state of nature, and many thought it possible to restore the social harmony of an imagined past, free of the turbulence, conflict, and inconvenience of a more modern polity with clashing interests and political divisions. Thus the state constitutions written during the Revolution not only established a new basis for legitimate authority;

they also represented efforts to put some kind of lid on the bubbling cauldron of social conflict that Independence had fired, to reassert the organic and corporate character of society, and to arrest the growing secularism, social pluralism, and economic diversity of the eighteenth century.[7]

In the wake of Independence constitutional issues were fought over as vigorously as other great public questions. Men differed sharply on how best to construct the "new secular order." Questions concerning the reach of representation and the scope of the franchise were hotly debated and variously resolved by constitution-makers in different states. Nor did the establishment of government on the basis of written instruments during and after the Revolution end these divisions. Pennsylvania offers the best but by no means the only example of how a constitution could remain a focal issue for partisan conflict for an extended period of time. Of more central importance, however, was the great emotional and philosophical capital that the Revolutionary generation invested in the notion of written constitutional arrangements. The revival of interest in party and a modern understanding of the role an organized opposition can play in free government would come only after a degree of "constitutional relaxation" began to set in. Only in later years would it become apparent that the Revolution and the republican forms of government it had generated had not produced a unified social order, but had ushered in an age of increasingly democratic and contentious politics that called for new institutions, of which the political party, and eventually the modern party system, would be leading examples.

> It is true that in some of the states there are parties and discords; but let us look back and ask if we were ever without them? Such will exist wherever there is liberty; and perhaps they help to preserve it. By the collision of different sentiments, sparks of truth are struck out, and political light is obtained. The different factions, which at present divide us, aim all at the public good; the differences are only about the various modes of promoting it. . . . Parties are therefore the common lot of humanity, and ours are by no means more mischievous or less beneficial than those of other countries, nations and ages, enjoying in the same degree the great blessing of political liberty.[8]

So argued the venerable Benjamin Franklin in a 1786 essay published mainly for the benefit of European critics of America during the so-called "critical period."[9] A remarkable commentary, Franklin's statement stands almost alone in the literature of the time as a solid defense of political parties. It went beyond what would become the Madisonian position that party was an evil though inevitable presence in political life, and it anticipated by fifty years the shift toward the acceptance of party as a positive good that occurred during the Jackson period.[10]

But Franklin's view of faction is especially interesting because it was retrospective as well as forward-looking. With it Franklin renewed, if only for a moment, a line of political thought that was developing at the end of the colonial period only to be lost in the ideological tumult of the Revolution. Almost thirty years before, the Reverend William Smith, provost of Philadelphia College, had written in the first issue of *The American Magazine and Monthly Chronicle for the British Colonies* (1757):

> [P]olitical evil, internal discords, and civil commotions, which threaten the dissolution of a state, are frequently no more than the efforts of the constitution to expel certain noxious principles, and the proper effect of them is to establish the public weal in a more vigorous, regular and permanent state. . . .
>
> [H]appy is the state which is informed by it in the requisite degree. Its operation is salutary; and the consideration of this has often lighted up the hopes of the patriot. . . .[11]

Smith's statement was not as isolated as Franklin's would be. For while he was not really discussing political organization as such, or openly advocating parties as a regular feature of free government, Smith was one among a number of writers who had begun to challenge the conventional notion that oppositional politics was emblematic of governmental decay.[12] What is puzzling is why this line of late colonial political thought seems to have dried up during the period of the Revolution and the early republic, to be revived only with difficulty in the next century, long after Franklin's unique, even idiosyncratic, commentary was virtually forgotten. One answer would seem to be that societies caught up in revoutionary change, political reconstruction, and state-building cannot afford the luxury of parties and party systems because success in revolution requires unity of purpose. Moreover, the reconstitution of authority is a process which may force suspension of the freedom to disagree politically.[13] Late-eighteenth-century writers would have understood and agreed with these ideas, the dominant anti-party philosophy to which most of them still subscribed having prepared them to embrace it.

It is nonetheless true that parties contributed very substantially to political development in Revolutionary America, and this was especially the case in Pennsylvania. Despite the absence of a formal party structure that would satisfy a modern theory of party, we can observe in Revolutionary Pennsylvania the workings of a political system with party-like elements. Printers and preachers disseminated political positions associated with particular groups, mass meetings were assembled with surprising efficiency, petitions and broadsides appeared as if on call with long columns of signatures appended, large numbers of voters turned out in crucial elections, and private societies communicated their political positions to key members of the government.[14]

Most historians agree that Pennsylvania was the most politically advanced of all the new American states.[15] Even as a proprietary colony Pennsylvania had experienced factional divisions and the usages and practices associated with proto-party devlopment.[16] The Pennsylvania party rivalries that emerged in the late 1770's, however, had their roots in the crisis of Independence itself, when radical and moderate Whigs divided over the question of whether or not the state Assembly should continue to exist once the Pennsylvania Provincial Conference had called for the gathering of a constitutional convention.[17] This convention met from July to September 1776, and the instrument it produced and which went into effect in March 1777 was considered to be the most radical state constitution of the period — proof to moderates of the dangers of political excess, but to political liberals a model of enlightened populist republicanism.[18]

The new constitution soon became the central issue around which party divisions formed, divisions already in evidence in the convention itself when twenty-three of the ninety-six delegates present refused to sign the final document, thereby triggering a newspaper war over its merits.[19] The enactment of a series of loyalty test-oath laws in the next several years seriously weakened the political position of the constitution's opponents, since many of their supporters in the electorate were disfranchised by these tests. At the same time, the test-oath issue deepened the split between the emerging contestants and pushed into the ranks of the anti-constitutionalists some groups with mixed opinions on the constitution itself.[20] Early in the spring of 1779 a third major issue — that of the reorganization of Philadelphia College, allegedly a nest of Anglican Loyalism[21] — sharpened political polarities to such an extent that the two coalitions felt bound to formalize their differences. The anti-test, pro-college anti-constitutionalists established the "Republican Society,"[22] while pro-test, anti-college supporters of the constitution changed the name of their original core group, the Whig Society or True Whigs, to the Constitutional Society.[23] For several years thereafter the two parties, known as Republicans and Constitutionalists, dominated the politics of the state of Pennsylvania. The Constitutionalists had control of the government in 1779 and 1780 and then again from 1784 to 1786. The Republicans briefly gained a clear majority in the Assembly as a result of an election victory in 1783 and then achieved a second and more decisive resurgence in 1786. By then wartime emotionalism had subsided, the Constitutionalist party had begun to disintegrate, and the weakening of the remaining test-oath laws had led to a surge of support for the Republicans as former nonjurors returned to the polls. But as the test-oath issue declined in importance new issues arose. The fight over the ratification of the federal Constitution and the movement to revise the state's constitution shattered the party alignments of the previous decade, and the first Pennsylvania party system came to an end.

Not surprisingly, there are some sharp differences among historians regarding Pennsylvania's political history in this period, but the question that seems to have elicited the most sustained attention concerns the nature of the support for the two parties in that state. The major line of analysis, going back to Charles Beard, has tended toward an explanation characterized by dichotomous rivalries between east and west, conservatives and radicals, rich and poor, and cosmopolitans and localists.[24] Two recent doctoral dissertations have exploded this simple dualistic approach, substituting for it a more complex picture that reveals multifarious differences among known leaders of the two political groups, and among leaders and followers alike a consistent correlation between party affiliation and ethnic and religious identity.[25] Analyses of election returns, the composition of the Assembly, and officeholding patterns demonstrate that "the ethnic-religious conflict transcended region and class and was the most salient characteristic of the contending political forces in Pennsylvania."[26]

In general, however, the fundamental question that historians have elected to answer has remained practically unchanged since the early twentieth century. The concern to identify precisely which social groups supported what party presupposes that parties act primarily as spokesmen for interest groups. Applying this definition, historians wishing to probe beneath surface appearances and discover the real sources of conflict have investigated the social composition of both the leaders and the supporters of early political parties. The trouble with this approach is that it has tended to minimize the importance of parties as independent variables and has pushed historians into efforts to "see through" party structures in order to uncover the hidden springs of political action. But parties and party systems are, after all, more than political representatives of coalitions of interests.[27] Clearly parties have much to do with interest representation, but their function is the more complex one of coordinating and correlating sets of interests with the public good as that good is defined by the party's particular program and ideology. And in a democratic revolutionary setting parties play even more significant roles. There is a need to establish the *legitimacy* of the new regime, to *integrate* new elites into positions of leadership, and to enlarge the scope of *participation* by activating or "mobilizing" groups formerly excluded from public life.[28]

In Revolutionary Pennsylvania the existence of a political system composed of groups that called themselves parties and acted like parties eased the transition from proprietary government to constitutional republic despite extensive institutional change. In that sense the Pennsylvania "parties" helped to establish the *legitimacy* of the new regime without attempting to destroy their opponents. To be sure, the exodus of Loyalists which took place when the British withdrew from Philadelphia in June 1778 did remove a major divisive element from Pennsylvania politics. Still, it is interesting to observe that no seizure of power by anything like a revolutionary junta was ever contemplated. The Constitutionalists would use test-oaths as an instrument for undercutting voter support for the Republicans, but they made no serious effort to proscribe the leadership of that party or to prevent Republicans from taking their seats in the Assembly or from arguing their case in the public press. In 1778, for example, the Constitutionalist majority in the Assembly permitted their Republican opponents to take an oath to defend popular liberties — in effect, a loyalty oath to the constitution — with the reservation that they, the Republicans, would work to change its fundamental provisions by constitutional means.[29] Moreover, the very fact that it was the focal issue between the parties helped to give the constitution and the political arrangements it inaugurated public visibility and acceptability, particularly since the Republicans, despite the hyperbole of their criticisms, continued to honor its ground rules.[30] By 1779 the Pennsylvania constitution had gained a high degree of legitimacy across broad segments of the population. In warning his subordinates against "falling into the current of party" General Nathaniel Greene observed that "the Constitution has been gradually gaining ground from first to last. The firm footing which it now appears to have got in the minds of the People induces me to think it but folly to oppose its progress."[31]

In regard to the *integration* of new leadership, it is now fairly clear that a significant transformation took place in officeholding patterns as a result of the Revolution. One study has shown a sizeable shift in the distribution of seats in the Pennsylvania Assembly after 1776 from English and Welsh Quakers and Anglicans to Scotch-Irish Presbyterians and German Reformed and Lutherans.[32] The membership of the Provincial Conference of county committees and the Constitutional Convention of 1776 also reflected the emergence of these new ethnic and religious groups. Presbyterians and other non-Quaker, non-Anglican delegates comprised 68 per cent of the conference and 74 per cent of the convention, while Quakers and Anglicans numbered less than 20 per cent of the delegates of known religious affiliation in each body. From an ethnic rather than a religious perspective, a similar preponderance of Scotch-Irish and Germans over delegates of English and Welsh extraction is visible.[33] Another study has demonstrated that the principal executive and judicial offices changed hands in Pennsylvania in the course of the Revolution to an extent equalled only by New York and Georgia. It is clear that the Revolution brought about the entry of a high proportion of new men into public life and government service.[34]

On the question of *participation*, while there does not seem to have been a dramatic expansion of the Pennsylvania electorate during the Revolution, there was a change in the quality of participation, especially among the large German segment of the population. The Revolution changed the participation of these new elements from a "supportive" to an "active" role.[35] The dominant Quakers had built bridges to the German community as early as the 1750's, but the Quaker leaders limited that relationship to the solicitation of votes at the elections. Growing disenchantment with Quaker military policies during the French and Indian War and the movement to establish a royal government in place of the Penn proprietorship in the 1760's detached the Germans from their traditional Quaker allies. By the time of the Revolution the political activation of the German population was well advanced, and the new Presbyterian-dominated Constitutionalist party attracted the support of that alienated group. Suffrage extension as such was rather limited, however. The question was much discussed, especially by radicals in the militia, but while the constitution of 1776 did liberalize voting by substituting a tax-paying qualification for a property test, both parties drew back from admitting vagabonds or bonded laborers to the polls, preferring a one-year residency requirement and some measure of economic independence as qualifications to vote. The Constitutionalists also applied the new test-oaths with sufficient vigor to cancel what otherwise would have been a modest increase in the overall size of the voting population. In any case, colonial electorates were already large, and in states such as Pennsylvania where the franchise question was debated the issue had more to do with the theory of voting than with answering any clamor for suffrage extension.[36]

In considering these "systemic" problems of legitimacy, integration, and participation in relation to party development at the time of the Revolution, we must remember that Pennsylvania enjoyed certain advantages during this period of rapid change. The "sequence" and "clustering" of issues favored the kind of moderate, competitive, and tolerant two-party system that emerged.[37] The legitimacy crisis occurred first, and while the state constitution caused deep and abiding divisions in Pennsylvania, the fact that the issues raised by that constitution were squarely confronted at the very outset of the Revolution prepared the ground for the settling of other pressing problems. In addition, it is important to recognize that the number of crises was limited. History accelerated at a moderate rate in Revolutionary Pennsylvania. There was no great social upheaval, wholesale redistribution of property, or class revolt.[38] Intimidation was used against forestallers, pacifists, and Loyalists, and emotions ran high at public meetings, which sometimes turned into public brawls. But the one outbreak of real violence over economic and class grievances — the Fort Wilson incident in October 1779 — is noteworthy because the militiamen who took to the streets did so as a last resort and only after months of patient pressure had failed to move the authorities to take effective action to stabilize prices.[39] That the Fort Wilson affair was a relatively isolated occurrence also indicates that the militia, with its statewide organization, its own leadership cadres, and its radical political ideology, was nonetheless willing to work within the political system. The militia resorted to controlled acts of intimidation as a spur rather than a challenge to the government, which in 1779 was in the hands of the Constitutionalists, the party the rank and file militiamen generally supported.

This examination of Pennsylvania's politics during the Revolutionary era demonstrates that the two parties, the Constitutionalists and the Republicans, themselves helped to resolve the immediate challenge to order and authority presented by the Revolution. These groups emerged because the preconditions for party development existed in Pennsylvania probably to a greater degree than elsewhere, and they succeeded in meeting the systemic crisis of revolution because the "political culture" of Pennsylvania provided a climate favorable to their growth.[40]

But if this was true, why was it not so perceived? Why were parties condemned so uniformly throughout this period?[41] Why did conventional anti-party ideology remain a powerful element of political thought? Why, indeed, did it gain such wide currency in Pennsylvania itself,[42] when the historical record, as outlined here, contradicts the argument that in time of war or revolution new states cannot afford the luxury of party divisions? Clearly the Pennsylvania experience suggests a different approach, for here party differences seemed to have fostered a sense of identity with the state that transcended disputes over men and measures.[43]

The answer, I believe, lies not in the fact of revolution but in the changed attitude toward constitutionalism that the Revolution promoted — here described as a change from constitutionalism as process to constitutional formalism. Colonial Americans understood that their freedoms and the liberalism of their political regimes were rooted in actual experience. That experience consisted of increasing religious toleration through the disestablishment of churches, an open and highly politicized press, rights in law at least equivalent to those enjoyed by Englishmen, and, finally, a contentious and competitive public life that in some provinces was becoming regularized in the form of party and faction.[44] To be sure, in the colonial period questions of constitutional structure and form did receive serious attention. England's putative model of mixed government remained the normative standard upon which speculations on basic issues finally turned. The seventeenth-century charters were often relied upon to counter executive and imperial policies that Americans opposed. But because they did not know that a revolution would provide the opportunity to reconstruct their political regimes from top to bottom, American politicians and political writers were more concerned with immediate problems than with grand constitutional theories or designs. There was, in the words of one historian, an "ephemeral character [to] many of the seemingly profound constitutional struggles of the first half of the [eighteenth] century."[45] For example, questions about the power of the colonial assemblies relative to provincial executives over the control and disbursement of funds, the appointment of officials, the conduct of Indian affairs, and the establishment of courts of law and courts of equity were among the problems that beset colonial politicians prior to the Revolution. We would call them constitutional questions, but the people who fought these battles only dimly perceived their constitutional implications. At stake was money, interest, and power, not constitutional principle. In another area, editors and printers challenged excessive pretensions to power by colonial assemblies, including the claimed privilege to silence critics. These publicists questioned prevailing legal doctrines regarding the limits of press freedom. They contributed to a gathering realization that rigid models of government, however well-balanced, were no guarantee against the abuse of power. Political writers had begun to challenge the conventionally negative attitude toward informal institutions such as the unlicensed press and the organized faction. These late colonial Americans had a dynamic view of constitutionalism. Above all, they understood that their freedom rested upon political action. Nowhere was this better expressed than in William Smith's 1757 defense of oppositional politics referred to earlier:

> ... [C]ollisions are more or less the fate of every state; ... they discover the defects and weak sides of a government to those who had delayed repairing and fortifying them, for no other reason than that they had not before the same opportunity of knowing them; ... they give a clearer insight into the constitution, make people examine and understand their rights and liberties, and thereby teach them where to stand upon their guard against attacks from abroad, as well as the no less dangerous reforms of pretended patriots at home.[46]

Smith likened these collisions to "a fever in the human body, the general intention of which is salutary ..." in that it served to expel what he called "the morbific matter, which has disordered the constitution, and to restore the animal machine to its wonted health and vigor." He warned against the possibility of excess in such conflict, a danger capable of destroying "the functions of some principal organs; or . . . [of bringing] on a dissolution of the whole fabric." Politics was for Smith an integral part of the constitutional system — a system which required the strong medicine of political conflict to keep the body politic wholesome and healthy. There was in Smith, as well as in other late colonial defenders of parties, a growing realization that organized political activity was a positive component of free government. The tentative position that parties and factions had gained in late colonial life and thought reflects a pervasive sense that constitutional stability was rooted in the processes rather than in the forms of government, and that real liberties were best secured by political vigilance.[47]

The Revolution arrested this promising development and produced a much more formalized notion of what constitutional government was all about. Amidst the turmoil of war, civic upheaval, economic distress, and social tension, Americans made the quest for first principles of constitutional order their premier objective. Our truly extraordinary preoccupation with written constitutions[48] — not only what they should say but also how and by whom they should be drawn and ratified — was fruitful because it enabled the new states to overcome their immediate crises of legitimacy, but the price paid for this success was a dramatic reversal in the American attitude toward constitutional formalism and political action.

The Revolution brought an end to one of the most positive developments in late colonial life and fostered an ambivalence toward organized politics that was to remain part of American political thought for many years.[49] The constitutionalists of the new era attempted to ground stable and legitimate authority in the bedrock of absolute, universal, even scientific principles of free government. Their task was to discover those timeless principles and to enact them into fundamental law.[50] Political freedom was not a subject to be taken lightly nor was it to be left to the caprices of popular political action. Instead, man's political "behavior" had to be conditioned and regulated by rigid mechanisms whose primary purpose was the achievement of freedom through order and the security of property.[51]

The emphasis was upon objectifiable entities — institutions, procedures, and functions of government—rather than on such subjective and chance elements as interest, leadership, and popular action. Above all, the men who participated in the founding of the American republic thought of themselves as architects who would build an edifice of freedom for all time.[52]

In such a highly formalized constitutional atmosphere there was no place for political parties. Parties represented forces in public life that were disorderly, resistent to controls, highly personal, and given to the pursuit of unpredictable and erratic purposes. The only legitimate institutions for collective action were those recognized in the constitutions themselves. Parties were a form of "private government" outside the official system and hence dangerous to it.[53] Not only did the constitutions enacted by most of the states and eventually by the new nation not countenance parties, but they actually established mechanisms designed to make parties unnecessary and even, in some cases, to render them inoperable where they appeared. To borrow Richard Hofstadter's efficient phrase, they were in a fundamental sense "constitutions against parties."[54] The constitutional formalism that was a permanent legacy of the Revolution led to a "sublimation of politics"[55] from which American political theory did not fully recover for at least a century.[56]

From the perspective of this transition in the American attitude toward constitutionalism there was little difference in the position of so-called radicals and conservatives. Both shared a common belief that good government and social happiness were to be secured through constitutional engineering, though they differed over how best to build the machine. Above all, both sides stressed the importance of a written constitution as a necessary check on the excesses of party. As Thomas Paine later wrote:

> All of these things [the excesses of the French Revolution] have followed from the want of a constitution; for it is the nature and intention of a constitution to *prevent governing by party,* by establishing a common principle that shall limit and control the power and impulse of party, and that says to all parties, *thus far shalt thou go and no further.* But in the absence of a constitution, men look entirely to party; and in-

stead of principle governing party, party governs principle.[57] (Italics in original.)

Democrats like Paine rejected the utility of parties because of a deep commitment to popular sovereignty and a desire to remove all impediments between the people's will and the people's government. Revolutionary populists like Paine believed that a genuinely representative regime would perfectly register the popular will and that parties would only encumber that process.

On the other side, moderate Whigs resisted the notion of parties because parties challenged the automatic deference that the people owed to their natural leaders and stimulated disobedience, insubordination, and incivility. For conservative republicans the task of statesmanship was to establish a constitution that would carefully spell out and balance the functional roles of well-differentiated governmental departments. Benjamin Rush, for example, argued that "all governments are safe and free in proportion as they are compounded in a certain degree, and on the contrary, that all governments are dangerous and tyrannical in proportion as they approach to simplicity."[58] In addition, for Whigs like Rush constitutions had to provide sufficient checks on the popular will by confining it to a single branch of a bicameral legislature and by maintaining property qualifications for officeholders if not also for voters.[59] Thus William Bingham, a director of the Bank of North America, a Pennsylvania republican, and later a United States senator, urged the adoption of bicameralism because "when a Second independent Branch . . . is instituted, there is a mutual Check established on each others Proceedings; and the Spirit of Party, which may exist in one of the Orders of Government, can do no Danger, whilst the other is unpolluted with it —"[60] Clearly the common assumption of conservatives and radicals alike was that their objectives could be achieved through constitutional manipulation. Both put their faith in the efficacy of constitutional forms rather than in the uncertainties of popular politics.[61] Both believed that the priority issue was the building of sound constitutional foundations for the good society. In short, both conservatives and radicals were *constitutional determinists*.

Thus the virtual disappearance during the Revolution of the

developing tolerance of parties, a tolerance much in evidence in the late colonial period, was not primarily owing to the exigencies of war and revolution. Nor was it evidence of a simple misperception of reality. Rather it represented the emergence of a new constitutional paradigm that rapidly came to dominate political thought and to obscure the potential role of political parties in a republican system of government. The prevailing conviction now was that with the discovery of the immutable principles of good government and their enactment into fundamental constitutional law political freedom could be safeguarded for all time. In such a regime political parties had no place.

On May 10, 1776, the Second Continental Congress resolved "that it be recommended to the respective assemblies and conventions of the United Colonies, where no government sufficient to the exigencies of their affairs have been hitherto established, to adopt such government as shall, in the opinion of the representatives of the people, best conduce to the happiness and safety of their constituents in particular, and America in general."[62] In part the resolution was a political stratagem designed by John Adams to build momentum for separation from Britain, particularly in the delegation from Pennsylvania, which still drew back from the precipice of Independence.[63] But the resolution of May 10 also signifies the reluctance of the Continental Congress to sail in the rough waters of radical politics without first securing a safe anchorage ahead. The old regime was not to be cast over the side until law and legitimate authority were well on their way to being re-established in the rebellious states. Thus May 10 is probably as important a date in our history as Independence Day itself, for on that day, in constitutional terms at least, the colonial period can be said to have come to an end as we embarked on a new course in our constitutional and political evolution. That evolution has been marked by a continuing anxiety over the place of parties in our politics, though parties of one kind or another have been with us since Independence, and in some cases even before. This ambivalence in our attitude toward party originates in the tension between political activism and constitutional determinism, a tension that has been one of the enduring products of the American Revolution.

Constitutional Formalism or the Politics of Virtue?: A Comment

Stephen E. Patterson

George Dargo again raises the interesting question as to why Americans of the Revolutionary period rejected political parties, at least in theory, despite their relatively favorable experience with partisan politics in the late colonial period. The answer, he suggests, lies in the Revolutionaries' conviction that written constitutions were better than parties at guaranteeing political freedom. Fixed principles arrested the development of the idea of party. One might ask, however, if constitutional formalism is a sufficient explanation. Pennsylvania, the focus of this paper, prepared its first state constitution in 1776, yet the latest pre-Revolutionary defense of partisanship Professor Dargo cites is dated 1757, almost a full twenty years earlier. Were there no positive arguments for partisanship in those two decades? If not, would we not have to look elsewhere than at constitutional formalism to understand how pro-party theory disappeared by the 1760's?

An approach not altogether contrary to Professor Dargo's might emphasize the emergence during the 1760's and 1770's of the Revolutionary ideology of republicanism which, perhaps more than any other factor, shaped the nature of the constitutions — both state and national — drawn up after Independence. Long before the Revolutionaries thought of embedding fundamental principles of natural law in their constitutions, they argued that their rights sprang from such principles. Furthermore, they stressed that all social and political relationships must be governed by these principles which they held to be fixed and immutable. The task of shaping those principles into "positive law," as they called it, was the essence of the legislative process. Politics of this sort was a kind of science, an exercise in discovery, and it required a cool objectivity. As long as men were looking for grand principles, they clearly could not be guided by their own private interest, the interest of their constituents, or the interest of a party. Their object must be the good of the whole or the general welfare, and it was assumed that the general welfare was properly served when decisions and laws conformed to grand principles objectively determined. In the rhetoric of English commonwealthmen and American republicans, such objectivity was the essence of "virtue." Individuals were virtuous when they perceived the natural order of things and modified their behavior to conform with it. Legislators were virtuous when they pursued their tasks in an objective and disinterested way. One might argue that it was this concept of virtue, rooted as it was in a static conception of law, which posed the most formidable obstacle to the acceptance of party in the Revolutionary period.[1] A party-free society was thus a deep-seated ideal long before the Revolutionaries came to the task of writing constitutions.

More practically, we perhaps should remind ourselves that whatever difficulty the Revolutionaries had with the theory of partisanship, they readily fell into party groupings both before 1776 and after. In colonial Pennsylvania, Quakers and Proprietary partisans hammered away at one another and even, as in 1766, seized upon imperial issues in their attempt to discredit the opposition. Furthermore, proponents of the 1776 constitution quickly found themselves opposed by a conservative, Philadelphia-based elite which organized itself into a "Republican" party and cast Pennsylvania politics into a partisan mold for years thereafter. Moreover, not all Americans became Revolutionaries, and whatever constraints republicanism may have placed on the political perceptions of some, there were others — neutrals, Tories, the "disaffected" — who may have viewed parties more positively.

In the case of Massachusetts, for example, Tories became strong advocates of partisanship during the Revolution. No less a Tory than Thomas Hutchinson wrote in 1765 that men were mistaken who imagined they could be perfectly objective in their political decisions. Their view of the public is always biased, he observed. "Perhaps the case is the same with some who are opposite to us in publick affairs, who vote quite different from us and are under insensible bias the other way. This consideration should tend to keep us from discontent & disturbance in our minds when measures are pursued contrary to what appears to us to be right. Possibly we may be mistaken."[2] By 1775 this tolerant view of opposing political forces had (perhaps in self-defense) become a Tory article of faith. Daniel Leonard, the Tory author of the "Massachusettensis" letters in the famous newspaper debate with John Adams's "Novanglus," put it bluntly: "Party is inseparable from a free state." Furthermore, he insisted that there was honesty and ability in each of the Massachusetts parties. Leonard had no difficulty perceiving the discrepancy that existed between what men said and what they did. "Each party professes disinterested patriotism,"[3] he pointed out, but that did not make them less partisan. If such sentiment could exist in Massachusetts, is it not conceivable that it had its counterparts elsewhere? In Pennsylvania, for example, should we look only at Patriot writings or also at those of numerous others who resisted Independence, or of those who rejected the state constitution of 1776 but remained to struggle for control of the state government? Constitutional formalism certainly did nothing to prevent these men from becoming vigorously partisan, as the papers of John Dickinson, Thomas Wharton,[4] and others vividly attest.

As for the Orin Libby-Charles Beard view that partisans represented social or economic interests, Professor Dargo makes some interesting comments. He reminds us that parties can be independent variables with the ability to develop leadership, organize participation, communicate ideas, and so on. This functional approach to politics, borrowed from political scientists, produces new insights into the workings of political parties, though there is the danger that we may end up reading back into the earliest parties characteristics that they did not have. But whatever the value of such an analysis, it shifts the focus away from the causes of parties to their effects. The progressive historians, despite limitations in their methods, did ask fundamental questions about the origins of parties and provided an answer that, at least in my view, was perfectly consistent with the eighteenth-century conception of the nature of parties. James Madison put it more lucidly than most in *Federalist* No. 10, but he really said no more than was already implicit in general usage: the politics of virtue was a politics above interest, while the politics of party was the politics of interest. Furthermore, when men of the time became more specific about what the "interests" were, they more often than not identified them with stock jobbers, or with farmers, merchants, or other economic and social groups.

In contrast, the approach adopted by Professor Dargo takes the edge off partisan conflict in Pennsylvania after 1776. By concentrating on the functional role of parties, he shows that the party system had a moderating effect on politics, that parties helped to resolve the challenge to order and authority, and that they thereby helped Pennsylvanians meet what he calls their "systemic crisis." These common accomplishments of the two parties then prepare us for the grander conclusion that, despite surface differences over men and measures, party tension helped build a unity of purpose in the new state. In short, parties contributed to the development of a consensus rather than to continuing conflict.

Yet can one be sure that it was the party system which served to get Pennsylvanians through their "systemic crisis" rather than some other unexplored factor, particularly when we consider that many other states did not enjoy the same level of partisan sophistication, and yet all seem to have managed to cope with their "systemic crises"? Does this configuration not bring us back to the old consensus view of the Revolution while obscuring the role parties played in shaping the Revolution through their conflict? Another approach, for example, might show how parties saw constitution-making as an opportunity to advance their own interests. While parties paid lip service to the idea that constitutions should eliminate partisanship, perhaps they really hoped that constitutions would eliminate the other party, or at least give the advantage in terms of representation or other provision to themselves. Such an approach would also concern itself with the deeper roots of conflict, or, in other words, would seek to explain where the parties came from and why. The search for causes may produce answers quite different from those of Libby and Beard, but at least the dispute would be fairly joined.

NOTES

Patricia U. Bonomi (Pages v-xi)

1. The words *party* and *faction* are used interchangeably in this volume; following eighteenth-century usage, they will identify — as noted on an earlier occasion — any group of men with a temporary common interest which assumed a stance in opposition to any other group of men with a temporary common interest.
2. Representative writers on each point of view are Carl L. Becker, *The History of Political Parties in the Province of New York, 1760-1776* (Madison, Wis., 1909); Robert E. Brown, *Middle-Class Democracy and the Revolution in Massachusetts, 1691-1780* (Ithaca, N.Y., 1955); Michael Zuckerman, *Peaceable Kingdoms: New England Towns in the Eighteenth Century* (New York, 1970); J.R. Pole, "Historians and the Problem of Early American Democracy," *American Historical Review,* 67 (1962), 626-46.
3. Jack P. Greene, *The Quest for Power: The Lower Houses of Assembly in the Southern Royal Colonies, 1689-1776* (Chapel Hill, N.C., 1963); Bernard Bailyn, *The Origins of American Politics* (New York, 1968); Stanley N. Katz, *Newcastle's New York: Anglo-American Politics, 1732-1753* (Cambridge, Mass., 1968); Alison Gilbert Olson, *Anglo-American Politics, 1660-1775* (London, 1973); Paul Lucas, "A Note on the Comparative Study of the Structure of Politics in Mid-Eighteenth-Century Britain and Its American Colonies," *William and Mary Quarterly,* 3rd ser., 28 (1971), 301-9.
4. Bailyn, *Origins of Politics,* 64.
5. A notable effort to organize parties into four categories appears in Jack P. Greene's essay "Changing Interpretations of Early American Politics," in Ray Allen Billington, ed., *The Reinterpretation of Early American History* (New York, 1968).
6. See, for example, Alfred F. Young, ed., *The American Revolution: Explorations in the History of American Radicalism* (DeKalb, Ill., 1976).
7. Bernard Friedman, "The Shaping of the Radical Consciousness in Provincial New York," *Journal of American History,* 56 (1970), 781-801; Patricia U. Bonomi, *A Factious People: Politics and Society in Colonial New York* (New York, 1971), esp. 281-83; James H. Hutson, *Pennsylvania Politics, 1746-1770* (Princeton, N.J., 1972); David S. Lovejoy, *Rhode Island Politics and the American Revolution, 1760-1776* (Providence, 1958); Ronald Hoffman, *A Spirit of Dissension: Economics, Politics, and the Revolution in Maryland* (Baltimore, 1973); Jackson Turner Main, *Political Parties Before the Constitution* (Chapel Hill, N.C. 1973).
8. Patricia U. Bonomi, "The Middle Colonies: Embryo of the New Political Order," in Alden T. Vaughan and George A. Billias, eds., *Perspectives on Early American History* (New York, 1973), esp. 81-92; Stephen E. Patterson, *Political Parties in Revolutionary Massachusetts* (Madison, Wis., 1973).

J. G. A. Pocock (Pages 1-12)

1. See Everitt's *The Community of Kent and the Great Rebellion* (Leicester,

1966), *The Local Community and the Great Rebellion* (London: Historical Association Pamphlets, 1969), and *Change in the Provinces: The Seventeenth Century* (Leicester, 1969). The special character of the Kent county community was discussed by Peter Laslett in "The Gentry of Kent in 1640," *Cambridge Historical Journal* (now *The Historical Journal*), 9:2 (1948), 148–64.

2. Clive Holmes, *The Eastern Association in the English Civil War* (Cambridge, 1974).

3. The most recent studies are J.S. Morrill, *The Revolt of the Provinces: Conservatives and Radicals in the English Civil War* (New York, 1976), which, by focusing upon local defense associations such as the "Clubmen" and setting limits to the sometimes exaggerated centralization of the New Model Army, depicts the localism and incoherence of the grassroots Civil War at its maximum; and Robert Ashton, *The English Civil War: Conservatism and Revolution, 1603-1649* (New York, 1978).

4. R.R. Walcott, *English Politics in the Early Eighteenth Century* (Oxford, 1956); J.H. Plumb, *The Growth of Political Stability in England, 1675-1725* (London, 1967); Geoffrey Holmes, *British Politics in the Age of Anne* (London,1967); Geoffrey Holmes and W.A. Speck, *The Divided Society: Parties and Politics in England, 1691-1716* (London, 1967).

5. Keith Feiling, *A History of the Tory Party, 1640-1714* (Oxford, 1924); Dennis Rubini, *Court and Country, 1688-1702* (London, 1967); Isaac F. Kramnick, *Bolingbroke and His Circle: The Politics of Nostalgia in the Age of Walpole* (Cambridge, Mass., 1968); H.T. Dickinson, *Bolingbroke* (London, 1970); J.G.A. Pocock, *The Machiavellian Moment: Florentine Political Thought and the Atlantic Republican Tradition* (Princeton, N.J., 1975).

6. See John Brewer, *Party Politics and Popular Ideology at the Accession of George III* (Cambridge, 1976); H.T. Dickinson, *Liberty and Property: Political Ideologies in 18th Century Britain* (London, 1977).

7. Bernard Bailyn, *The Ideological Origins of the American Revolution* (Cambridge, Mass., 1967), and *The Origins of American Politics* (New York, 1968); Gordon S. Wood, *The Creation of the American Republic, 1776-1787* (Chapel Hill, N.C., 1969); Gerald Stourzh, *Alexander Hamilton and the Idea of Republican Government* (Stanford, Calif., 1970); J.G.A. Pocock, "Virtue and Commerce in the Eighteenth Century," *Journal of Interdisciplinary History*, 3:1 (1972), 119–34.

8. Louis B. Hartz, ed., *The Founding of New Societies* (New York, 1954).

9. See Paul Lucas, "A Note on the Comparative Study of the Structure of Politics in Mid-Eighteenth-Century Britain and Its American Colonies," *William and Mary Quarterly*, 3rd ser., 28 (1971), 301–9.

10. For this ideological duality, see Pocock, *The Machiavellian Moment*, chaps. XIII-XIV; Bernard Bailyn, *The Ordeal of Thomas Hutchinson* (Cambridge, Mass., 1974); Duncan Forbes, *Hume's Philosophical Politics* (Cambridge, 1976).

11. William N. Chambers, *Political Parties in a New Nation: The American Experience, 1776-1809* (New York, 1963); Richard Hofstadter, *The Idea of a Party System: The Rise of Legitimate Opposition in the United States, 1780-1840* (Berkeley, Calif., 1969).

12. Wood, *Creation of the American Republic*.

13. See John W. Shy, *A People Numerous and Armed* (New York, 1976).

14. See Lance Banning, *The Jeffersonian Persuasion: Evolution of a Party Ideology* (Ithaca, N.Y., 1978).

15. For example, David Hackett Fischer, *The Revolution of American Conservatism* (New York, 1965); Richard Buel, Jr., *Securing the Revolution: Ideology in American Politics, 1789-1815* (Ithaca, N.Y., 1972).
16. See John M. Murrin, "The Great Inversion, or Court v. Country: a Comparison of the Revolution Settlements in England (1688-1721) and America (1776-1816)," in J.G.A. Pocock, ed., *Three British Revolutions: 1641, 1688, 1776* (Princeton, NJ, 1980).

Stephen Botein (Pages 13-34)

The author wishes to thank William La Piana for valuable assistance researching sections of this essay.

1. Benjamin Church, *An Oration, Delivered . . . to Commemorate the Bloody Tragedy of the Fifth of March, 1770* (Boston, 1773), 17-18.
2. The importance of socio-political harmony in New England, especially as an ideal at the local level, is discussed by Michael Zuckerman in *Peaceable Kingdoms: New England Towns in the Eighteenth Century* (New York, 1970), chaps. 2,7; and see Stephen E. Patterson, *Political Parties in Revolutionary Massachusetts* (Madison, Wis., 1973), chap. 1.
3. [John Allen], *An Oration, Upon the Beauties of Liberty . . .* (Boston, 1773), x. On habits of constitutional discourse in eighteenth-century New England, see generally T.H. Breen, *The Character of the Good Ruler: A Study of Puritan Political Ideas in New England, 1630-1730* (New Haven, 1970), chaps. 5-7; John Phillip Reid, "In a Defensive Rage: The Uses of the Mob, the Justification in Law, and the Coming of the American Revolution," *New York University Law Review*, 49 (1974), 1050-67.
4. See, for example, historiographical comments by David H. Flaherty, "An Introduction to Early American Legal History," in Flaherty, ed., *Essays in the History of Early American Law* (Chapel Hill, N.C., 1969), 17; Milton M. Klein, "New York Lawyers and the Coming of the American Revolution," *New York History*, 55 (1974), 383-407.
5. The specificity of English jurists is remarked by M.I. Finley in *The Ancestral Constitution: An Inaugural Lecture* (Cambridge, 1971), 22-23. According to Ernest Barker, "Natural Law and the American Revolution," in *Traditions of Civility: Eight Essays* (Cambridge, 1948), 295, the colonists "failed to make their case good" upon a "theory of the English constitution which begins from a consideration of the rights of the subject under that constitution." The recent understanding of law in Revolutionary American thought is presented most influentially in Bernard Bailyn, *The Ideological Origins of the American Revolution* (Cambridge, Mass., 1967), esp. 30-31 and chap. 5.
6. Among the relevant titles published approximately half a century ago are the following: Carl L. Becker, *The Declaration of Independence: A Study in the History of Ideas* (New York, 1922); Benjamin Fletcher Wright, Jr., *American Interpretations of Natural Law: A Study in the History of Political Thought* (Cambridge, Mass., 1931); Charles F. Mullett, *Fundamental Law and the American Revolution, 1760-1776* (New York, 1933). Also originating in the same period were Edward S. Corwin's *The "Higher Law" Background of American Constitutional Law* (Ithaca, N.Y., 1955), which first appeared in the *Harvard Law Review* of 1928-29, and Barker,

"Natural Law and the American Revolution," initially prepared in 1929 for the Lowell Lecture series in Boston. One reason scholars in the 1920's and 1930's were interested in early American theories of natural law, it appears, was that similar theories could be said to have informed conservative judicial decision-making in the decades between Reconstruction and the New Deal. The theme of subsequent use—and misuse—by "reactionary" judges was developed most elaborately in Charles Grove Haines, *The Revival of Natural Law Concepts* (Cambridge, Mass., 1930).

7. Douglass Adair and John A. Schutz, eds., *Peter Oliver's Origin & Progress of the American Rebellion: A Tory View* (San Marino, Calif., 1963), 42. Wright (*American Interpretations of Natural Law*, 75) states a common view when he identifies polemicists in New England as the "leaders in spreading the gospel of the inherent rights derived from the laws of nature." A good example of the Jeffersonian perspective, on the other hand, may be found in Henry Steele Commager, *The Empire of Reason: How Europe Imagined and America Realized the Enlightenment* (Garden City, N.Y., 1977), chap. 6.

8. Assumptions along these lines appear to underlie such discussions as R.A. Humphreys, "The Rule of Law and the American Revolution," *Law Quarterly Review*, 53 (1937), 87; Thad W. Tate, "The Social Contract in America, 1774-1787: Revolutionary Theory as a Conservative Instrument," *William and Mary Quarterly*, 3rd ser., 22 (1965), 376-78; Donald H. Meyer, *The Democratic Enlightenment* (New York, 1976), 100-04. The unstated premise of Richard B. Morris in "Legalism versus Revolutionary Doctrine in New England," *New England Quarterly*, 4 (1931), 195-215, is that natural rights theory consisted of extralegal doctrine—above and beyond "reactionary" legal reasoning.

9. *Oliver's Origin & Progress of the American Rebellion*, 41-43; and see, for examples, Charles J. Stillé, *The Life and Times of John Dickinson* (Philadelphia, 1891), 24-34; John G. Buchanan, "Drumfire from the Pulpit: Natural Law in the Colonial Election Sermons of Massachusetts," *American Journal of Legal History*, 12 (1968), 232-44; Paul K. Conkin, *Self-Evident· Truths* (Bloomington, Ind., 1974), 103-5, 107. The most useful study remains Alice M. Baldwin, *The New England Clergy and the American Revolution* (Durham, N.C., 1928), where it is claimed that in the decades preceding the Revolutionary period the ministers of New England "preserved, extended, and popularized" doctrines of natural rights and social contract dating from the seventeenth century (p. xii).

10. According to Bernard Bailyn, in "Religion and Revolution: Three Biographical Studies," *Perspectives in American History*, 4 (1970), 96-97, the sermon literature of New England provided the broad "substratum of belief that underlay the developing rebellion." Despite Alan E. Heimert's suggestion in *Religion and the American Mind from the Great Awakening to the Revolution* (Cambridge, Mass., 1966), 240-42, there is no reason to identify natural rights theory primarily as the political language of the Arminian clergy.

11. Bailyn, *Ideological Origins*, 26-30; and see John Dunn, "The politics of Locke in England and America in the eighteenth century," in John W. Yolton, ed., *John Locke: Problems and Perspectives* (Cambridge, 1969), 74-76. Reid, "In a Defensive Rage," 1060-61, offers an especially telling example of Tory reliance upon natural rights argumentation.

12. For theoretical discussion of issues relating to the general methodological

approach followed here, see Quentin Skinner, "Meaning and Understanding in the History of Ideas," *History and Theory,* 8 (1969), 3-53; and J.G.A. Pocock, *Politics, Language and Time: Essays on Political Thought and History* (New York, 1971), chap. 1.

13. Some elements of the argument that follows may be found, incomplete, in Richard Hofstadter, *America at 1750: A Social Portrait* (New York, 1971), chaps. 6-8; see Stanley Elkins and Eric McKitrick, "Richard Hofstadter: A Progress," in Elkins and McKitrick, eds., *The Hofstadter Aegis: A Memorial* (New York, 1974), 365-67. Relevant sociological theory is available in Peter L. Berger and Thomas Luckmann, *The Social Construction of Reality: A Treatise in the Sociology of Knowledge* (Garden City, N.Y., 1966).

14. James Otis, "The Rights of the British Colonies Asserted and proved" (Boston, 1764), reprinted in Bernard Bailyn, ed., *Pamphlets of the American Revolution: 1750-1776* (Cambridge, Mass., 1965), I, 436-37; and see generally Mullett, *Fundamental Law,* chaps. 1-2. The influence of Scottish philosophers, particularly Francis Hutcheson, should also be noted; but this strain does not appear to have been as prominent in the literature under examination here as it was in Jefferson's thinking, as interpreted by Garry Wills in *Inventing America: Jefferson's Declaration of Independence* Garden City, N.Y., 1978).

15. William Patten, *A Discourse Delivered at Hallifax*...(Boston, 1766), 17. Dunn, "The politics of Locke," 45-80, discounts Locke's importance, as does Ronald E. Pynn, "The Influence of John Locke's Political Philosophy on American Political Tradition," *North Dakota Quarterly,* 42 (1974), 48-56. Whether or not the *Two Treatises* made much of an impact on many Americans, however, Locke was definitely the most illustrious name in the roster of natural rights theorists that Revolutionary leaders in New England *said* had influenced their thought.

16. Christopher Hill, "'Reason' and 'reasonableness' in seventeenth-century England," *British Journal of Sociology,* 20 (1969), 235-52. Without specifically analyzing natural rights theory, Pauline Maier discusses this same literature in *From Resistance to Revolution: Colonial Radicals and the Development of American Opposition to Britain, 1765-1776* (New York, 1972), chap. 2.

17. What follows is a kind of composite reconstruction of Revolutionary logic in New England, based on readings of publications listed in Thomas R. Adams, *American Independence: The Growth of an Idea* (Providence, 1965). Because Adams is rather selective (p. xiv) in including religious materials, I have made a limited effort to supplement his bibliography. Most of the works cited below have no intrinsic importance; they are meant merely to be representative of argumentative patterns in the Revolutionary literature.

18. Ebenezer Bridges, *A Sermon Preached before His Excellency Francis Bernard*... (Boston, 1767), 17; Stephen Johnson, *Integrity and Piety the best Principles of a good Administration of Government* ... (New London, Conn., 1770), 7; [Moses Mather], *America's Appeal to the Impartial World* (Hartford, 1775), 65; Charles Francis Adams, ed., *The Works of John Adams* (Boston, 1856), IV, 15; John Hancock, *An Oration; Delivered*... *to Commemorate the Bloody Tragedy of the Fifth of March 1770* (Boston, 1774), 6.

19. Bridges: *Sermon,* 18; Church, *Oration,* 9; Josiah Stearns, *Two Sermons*

Preached at Epping . . . (Newburyport, Mass., 1777), 15; John Allen, *The American Alarm, Or The Bostonian Plea, For the Rights, and Liberties, of the People* (Boston, 1773), 5-6.

20. Benjamin Trumbull, *A Discourse, Delivered at the Anniversary Meeting of the Freemen of the Town* . . . (New Haven, 1773), 13, 30.
21. See, for example, Gordon S. Wood, *The Creation of the American Republic, 1776-1787* (Chapel Hill, N.C., 1969), chap. 1, esp. 6-8, where laws of morality and laws of behavior are not sharply distinguished; the line is drawn more clearly by C.N. Stockton in "Three Enlightenment Variations of Natural Law Theory," *Enlightenment Essays*, I (1970), 127-31. One French mode of thinking, quite different from that prevailing in New England, is described in John Arthur Mourant, *The Physiocratic Conception of Natural Law* (Chicago, 1943). For an excellent theoretical discussion of natural law and related problems in eighteenth-century political thought, at a level seldom reached by Revolutionary polemicists in New England, see Morton White, *The Philosophy of the American Revolution* (New York, 1978).
22. Jonathan Williams Austin, *An Oration, Delivered . . . to Commemorate the Bloody Tragedy of the Fifth of March* . . . (Boston, 1778), 5.; Johnson, *Integrity and Piety*, 25.
23. Bridges, *Sermon*, 17-18; *A Discourse, Addressed to Sons of Liberty* . . . (Providence, 1766), 1.
24. Samuel West, *A Sermon Preached before the Honorable Council, and the Honorable House of Representatives* . . . (Boston, 1776), 11; Daniel Shute, *A Sermon Preached before His Excellency Francis Bernard* . . . (Boston, 1768), 12, 16-17; Patten, *Discourse*, 11.
25. Edward Barnard, *A Sermon Preached before His Excellency Francis Bernard* . . . (Boston, 1766), 26, 17; [Stephen Johnson], *Some Important Observations, Occasioned by, and adapted to, The Public Fast* (Newport, 1776), 10.
26. [Silas Downer], *A Discourse Delivered in Providence* . . . (Providence, 1768), 6; John Tucker, *A Sermon Preached . . . before His Excellency Thomas Hutchinson* . . . (Boston, 1771), 43. On the appeal of *Calvin's Case*, see Charles F. Mullett, "Coke and the American Revolution," *Economica*, 12 (1932), 462.
27. Samuel Sherwood, *A Sermon, Containing, Scriptural Instructions to Civil Rulers, and all Free-born Subjects* (New Haven, 1774), 31; Ebenezer Baldwin, "Appendix," *ibid.*, 58; [Downer], *Discourse*, 10-11. Whatever the merits of C.B. Macpherson's "bourgeois" interpretation of Lockean thought, as in *The Political Theory of Possessive Individualism; Hobbes to Locke* (Oxford, 1962), it seems less applicable to natural rights proponents in New England than to those in the mother country, where presumably the conditions of a "possessive market society" were far more highly developed. Similarly, the "individualistic" emphasis of Cecelia M. Kenyon in "The Declaration of Independence," in *Fundamental Testaments of the American Revolution* (Washington, 1973), 32-33, seems inappropriate within the communal context of late Puritan thought.
28. Amos Adams, *Religious Liberty an invaluable Blessing* . . . (Boston, 1768), 7; Israel Holly, *God brings about his holy and wise Purpose* . . . (Hartford, 1774), 17; Samuel Baldwin, *A Sermon, Preached at Plymouth* . . . (Boston, 1776), 14; Eleazar Wheelock, *Liberty of Conscience* . . .

(Hartford, 1776), 16; Judah Champion, *Christian and Civil Liberty and Freedom Considered and Recommended* . . . (Hartford, 1776), 6.

29. Patten, *Discourse*, 12; Tucker, *Sermon*, 5; Johnson, *Integrity and Piety*, 5; Shute, *Sermon*, 20-21. Within this context, it might be added, the mood of the Declaration of Independence could be said to have been somewhat more Protestant than Henry F. May suggests in *The Enlightenment in America* (New York, 1976), 162-63. G.B. Warden, in "The Revolutionary Origins of Law in New England" (unpublished paper), speculates intriguingly that multilateral social contract theory in New England was rooted in the seventeenth-century Puritan practice of drawing up civil covenants.

30. Andrew Eliot, *A Sermon Preached before His Excellency Francis Bernard* . . . (Boston, 1765), 21; Jonathan Lee, *A Sermon, Delivered before the General Assembly* . . . (New London, 1766), 14.

31. Stearns, *Two Sermons*, 12; Nathaniel Niles, *Two Discourses on Liberty* . . . (Newburyport, Mass., 1774), 23-24n; West, *Sermon*, 14; Shute, *Sermon*, 20-21.

32. [John, Lord Somers], *The Judgment of Whole Kingdoms and Nations, Concerning the Rights, Power and Prerogative of Kings* . . . (Boston, 1773), 36, 79. Although there is uncertainty as to the authorship of this tract, as indicated by Caroline Robbins, *The Eighteenth-Century Commonwealthman* (Cambridge, Mass., 1959), 78-80, its importance to Revolutionary Americans is indisputable. Editions appeared in Philadelphia, New York, and Newport as well as Boston.

33. Peter Thacher, *An Oration Delivered* . . . *to Commemorate the Bloody Massacre at Boston* . . . (Watertown, Mass., 1776), 8; Resolutions, Massachusetts House of Representatives, Oct. 29, 1765, in H.A. Cushing, ed., *The Writings of Samuel Adams* (New York, 1904-8), I, 23-24.

34. The issue was debated explicitly, with Locke cited on both sides, in Thomas Hutchinson, "A Dialogue between an American and a European Englishman [1768]." Bernard Bailyn, ed., *Perspectives in American History*, 9 (1975), 343-410.

35. *Works of John Adams*, IV, 15.

36. See J.W. Gough, *Fundamental Law in English Constitutional History* (Oxford, 1955), chaps. 11-12. According to Gordon J. Schochet, *Patriarchalism in Political Thought: The Authoritarian Family and Political Speculation and Attitudes Especially in Seventeenth-Century England* (New York, 1975), 81-84, contractual thinking had never been widely popular in the mother country.

37. For example, Joseph Emerson quoted Cotton Mather to this effect in *A Thanksgiving-Sermon Preach'd at Pepperrell* . . . (Boston, 1766), 28; see generally Wright, *American Interpretations of Natural Law*, 38-40; and Mullett, *Fundamental Law*, 66-67. It may well be, however, that in New England the experience and memory of the Glorious Revolution helped sustain subsequent interest within the region in Lockean theory; see Theodore B. Lewis, "A Revolutionary Tradition, 1689-1774; 'There Was a Revolution Here As Well As in England,' " *New England Quarterly*, 46 (1973), 424-38.

38. James Lovell, *An Oration Delivered* . . . *to Commemorate the Bloody Tragedy of the Fifth of March, 1770* (Boston, 1771), 17. The discrepancy between form and reality in the empire is a major theme of Bernard Bailyn, *The Origins of American Politics* (New York, 1968). Suggestions

that this discrepancy was reflected in rival modes of constitutional discourse are to be found in Reid, "In a Defensive Rage," 1087; and Breen, *Character of the Good Ruler,* chaps. 6-7. Although the latter associates the established Congregational clergy with "Court" values, he also remarks on the congruence of "Country" and traditional Puritan thinking.

39. See Daniel J. Boorstin, *The Americans: The Colonial Experience* (New York, 1958), chaps. 31-33. Within the legal profession itself, however, leading Patriot ideologues were apt to be highly professional in their aspirations, according to John M. Murrin, "The Legal Transformation: The Bench and Bar of Eighteenth-Century Massachusetts," in Stanley N. Katz, ed., *Colonial America: Essays in Politics and Social Development* (Boston, 1971), 415-49.

40 This is Mullett's premise in *Fundamental Law,* 73, for example; doubtless there was some such intellectual continuity, but one would expect the higher law traditions to have become attenuated in the absence of supporting eighteenth-century circumstances.

41. Cotton Mather, *A Monitory Letter About the Maintenance of an Able and Faithful Ministry* (Boston, 1700), 3. A good overview of the clergy in eighteenth-century New England is available in Donald M. Scott, *From Office to Profession: The New England Ministry, 1750-1850* (Philadelphia, 1978), chap. 1; for further information, see John William Youngs, Jr., *God's Messengers: Religious Leadership in Colonial New England, 1700-1750* (Baltimore, 1976); and James W. Schmotter, "Ministerial Careers in Eighteenth Century New England: The Social Context, 1700-1760," *Journal of Social History,* 9 (1975-76), 249-67.

42. Thomas Symmes, *The People's Interest . . . Consider'd & Exhibited . . .* (Boston, 1724), 4; Clifford K. Shipton, *Biographical Sketches of Those Who Attended Harvard College . . .* (Cambridge and Boston, 1933-75), VII, 430.

43. Jonathan Mayhew, *A Sermon Preach'd in the Audience of His Excellency William Shirley . . .* (Boston, 1754), 15, 50.

44. [John Cleaveland et al.], *A Plain Narrative Of the Proceedings which caused The Separation . . .* (Boston, 1747), 3-4; a detailed account of this episode may be found in Christopher M. Jedrey, "The World of John Cleaveland: Family and Community in Eighteenth-Century Massachusetts" (Ph.D. diss., Harvard University, 1977), chap. 2. Whether individuals might withdraw, without group sanction, was unclear. On the theory of separation, see C.C. Goen, *Revivalism and Separatism in New England, 1740-1800: Strict Congregationalists and Separate Baptists in the Great Awakening* (New Haven, 1962), 58-67.

45. Ebenezer Gay, *Ministers Insufficiency for their important and difficult Work . . .* (Boston, 1742),17; Ebenezer Gay, *The true Spirit of a Gospel-Minister represented, and urged* (Boston, 1746), 20; Charles Chauncy, *Ministers cautioned against the Occasions of Contempt* (Boston, 1744), 19.

46. Jonathan Mayhew, *Seven Sermons . . .* (Boston, 1749), 56; Ebenezer Gay, *The Alienation of Affections from Ministers . . .* (Boston, 1747), 13; Ebenezer Gay, *A Call from Macedonia* (Boston, 1768), 14-15.

47. Thomas Clap, *A Brief History and Vindication of the Doctrines Received and Established in the Churches of New-England . . .* (New Haven, 1755), 23-24; the local political background of this publication is described suc-

cinctly in Richard L. Bushman, *From Puritan to Yankee: Character and the Social Order in Connecticut, 1690-1765* (Cambridge, Mass., 1967), 241-53. For the outlook of London dissent, see Carl Bridenbaugh, *Mitre and Sceptre: Transatlantic Faiths, Ideas, Personalities, and Politics, 1689-1775* (New York, 1962), 46-47.

48. Charles Chauncy, *The only Compulsion proper to be made Use of in the Affairs of Conscience and Religion* (Boston, 1739), 9; Charles Chauncy, *Seasonable Thoughts on the State of Religion in New England . . .* (Boston, 1743), 367; Elisha Williams, "The essential Rights and Liberties of Protestants" (Boston, 1744) in Alan E. Heimert and Perry Miller, eds., *The Great Awakening: Documents Illustrating the Crisis and Its Consequences* (New York, 1967), 324.

49. Charles Chauncy, *A Letter to a Friend . . .* (Boston, 1767), 26; and see generally Nathan O. Hatch, "The Origins of Civil Millenialism in America: New England Clergymen, War with France, and the Revolution," *William and Mary Quarterly*, 3rd ser., 31 (1974), 423-25.

50. Ebenezer Gay, *St. John's Vision of the Woman cloathed with the Sun . . .* (Boston, 1766), 31; Goen, *Revivalism and Separatism*, 67n.

51. See, for example, West, *Sermon*, 21; Tucker, *Sermon*, 16; Chauncy, *Letter*, 47.

52. Thomas Paine, *Common Sense and The Crisis* (Garden City, N.Y., 1973), 34; and see Bernard Bailyn, "Common Sense," in *Fundamental Testaments*, 21-22, where Paine's relationship to Puritan culture is noted.

53. Essex *Gazette*, Apr. 25, 1775; Jonathan Mayhew, *A Letter of Reproof to Mr. John Cleaveland . . .* (Boston, 1764), 26; Jonathan Mayhew, "A Discourse Concerning Unlimited Submission and Non-Resistance to the Higher Powers . . ." (Boston, 1750), in Bailyn, ed., *Pamphlets of the American Revolution*, I, 241. And see Charles W. Akers, *Called unto Liberty: A Life of Jonathan Mayhew, 1720-1766* (Cambridge, Mass., 1964), 131-32; Jedrey, "World of John Cleaveland," chap. 4; Stephen Botein, "Rationalism, Constitutional Theory, and the Great Awakening in New England, 1735-1776" (senior thesis, Harvard College, 1963).

54. [Allen], *American Alarm*, 13-14, 7, 15; and see John M. Bumsted and Charles E. Clark, "New England's Tom Paine: John Allen and the Spirit of Liberty," *William and Mary Quarterly*, 3rd ser., 21 (1964), 561-70; Gad Hitchcock, *A Sermon Preached before His Excellency Thomas Gage . . .* (Boston, 1774), 34, 21.

55. Amos Adams, *A concise, historical view of the perils, hardships, difficulties and discouragements . . .* (Boston, 1769), 27; Adams, *Religious Liberty*, 25; Edward Bancroft, *Remarks on the Review of the Controversy . . .* (New London, 1771), 81. Bancroft's argument, originally published two years earlier in London, was relatively cautious in it assumption that the colonists had been granted title to their American lands by James I and Charles I. For a helpfully suggestive discussion of Lockean and Puritan themes in this context, see Michael Kammen, "The Meaning of Colonization in American Revolutionary Thought," *Journal of the History of Ideas*, 31 (1970), 337-58. In some respects, it appears, New Englanders anticipated certain issues concerning citizenship that became of acute interest following 1776, as indicated by James H. Kettner in "The Development of American Citizenship in the Revolutionary Era: The Idea of Volitional Allegiance," *American Journal of Legal History*, 18 (1974), 208-42.

56. Jason Haven, *A Sermon Preached before his Excellency Sir Francis Bernard* . . . (Boston, 1769), 45; Judah Champion, *A Brief View of the Distresses* . . . *Our Ancestors Encounter'd* . . . (Hartford, 1770), 31; *A Brief Review of the Rise, Progress, Services and Sufferings of New-England* (Norwich, Conn., 1774), 6 (originally published in England); Patten, *Discourse*, 15; Adams, *Religious Liberty*, 53. For the relevant sections of the earlier argument in a Revolutionary edition, see Jeremiah Dummer, *A Defence of the New-England Charters* (Boston, 1765), 1-9.
57. [Samuel Mather], *An Attempt to Shew, That America Must Be Known to the Ancients* . . . (Bostón, 1773), "Appendix," 32; Charles Chauncy, *A Discourse on "the good News from a far Country"* (Boston, 1766), 14, 20-21; Church, *Oration*, 12; Adams, *Religious Liberty*, 53; Baldwin, *Sermon*, 14-15, 22-23; Henry Cumings, *A Sermon, Preached in Billerica* . . . (Worcester, Mass., 1776), 23.
58. Essex *Gazette*, Mar. 26, Apr. 9, 1771; Apr. 25, 1775.
59. William Gordon, *The Separation of the Jewish Tribes, After the Death of Solomon* . . . (Boston, 1777), 22-23; Nicholas Street, *The American States Acting Over the Part of the Children of Israel in the Wilderness* . . . (New Haven, 1777), 10.
60. Robert P. Hay, "George Washington: American Moses," *American Quarterly*, 21 (1969), 780-91. Such writers as Barker, "Natural Law and the American Revolution," 330-55; and Haines, *Revival of Natural Law Concepts*, esp. chaps. 4-5, suggest the persistence of natural rights theory in both constitutional and civil law, but there is little doubt that it seldom functioned again as it had in the Revolutionary era. See, for example, Tate, "Social Contract in America," 386-91; Conkin, *Self-Evident Truths*, 122-28.
61. See generally Wood, *Creation of the American Republic.*
62. Benjamin Hichborn, *An Oration, Delivered* . . . *to Commemorate the Bloody Tragedy of the Fifth of March* (Boston, 1777), 5.

Stanley N. Katz (Pages 35-42)

1. New vigor has been introduced into the intellectual history of the Revolution by Garry Wills, who emphasizes the Scottish "common sense" philosophical tradition, and by Morton White, who has deepened our understanding of the Lockean tradition. Garry Wills, *Inventing America: Jefferson's Declaration of Independence* (Garden City, N.Y., 1978); Morton White, *The Philosophy of the American Revolution* (New York, 1978).
2. Becker: New York, 1922; Adams: Durham, N.C., 1922.
3. Declaration of Independence, in Richard L. Perry and John C. Cooper, eds., *Sources of our Liberties* (Chicago, rev. ed., 1978), 319.
4. Morison: New York, 1923.
5. Davidson: Chapel Hill, N.C., 1941.
6. Bailyn: Cambridge, Mass., 1967; Wood: Chapel Hill, N.C., 1969.
7. Caroline Robbins, *The Eighteenth-Century Commonwealthman* (Cambridge, Mass., 1959).
8. Henry St. John, Viscount Bolingbroke, for whom see Isaac F. Kramnick, *Bolingbroke and His Circle: The Politics of Nostalgia in the Age of Walpole* (Cambridge, Mass., 1968).
9. John Trenchard and Thomas Gordon, for whom see Robbins, *Com-

monwealthman, 115-25.
10. Baldwin: Durham, N.C., 1928.
11. Bernard Bailyn, "Religion and Revolution: Three Biographical Studies," Perspectives in American History, 4 (1970), 85-139.
12. Jonathan Mayhew, "A Discourse Concerning Unlimited Submission and Non-Resistance to the Higher Powers . . ." (Boston, 1750), in Bernard Bailyn, ed., Pamphlets of the American Revolution, 1750-1776 (Cambridge, Mass., 1965), I, 213-47; [John Joachim Zubly], An Humble Enquiry into the Nature of the Dependency of the American Colonies . . . (Charleston, 1769); [Jonathan Boucher], A Letter from a Virginian, to the Members of the Congress . . . (New York, 1774).
13. Heimert: Cambridge, Mass., 1966. See also Alan E. Heimert and Perry Miller, eds., The Great Awakening (Indianapolis, 1967), xiii-lxi; Sidney E. Mead, "American Protestantism during the Revolutionary Epoch," Church History, 22 (1953).
14. See Perry Miller, Errand into the Wilderness (Cambridge, Mass., 1956), and The New England Mind: From Colony to Province (Cambridge, Mass., 1953).
15. McIlwain: New York, 1923. See also Charles H. McIlwain, Constitutionalism Ancient and Modern (Ithaca, N.Y., rev. ed., 1947).
16. Schuyler: New York, 1929.
17. Charles Grove Haines, The Revival of Natural Law Concepts (Cambridge, Mass. 1930); Benjamin Fletcher Wright, Jr., American Interpretations of Natural Law: A Study in the History of Political Thought (Cambridge, Mass., 1931); Charles F. Mullett, Fundamental Law and the American Revolution, 1760-1776 (New York, 1933); Edward S. Corwin, The "Higher Law" Background of American Constitutional Law (Ithaca, N.Y., 1955).
18. As Botein has noted (footnote 6), scholarly interest in the natural law aspects of the Revolutionary movement seems clearly linked to criticism of the substantive due process orientation of the United States Supreme Court in the 1920's. The reaction against the apparently subjective behavior of the Court impelled scholars to re-examine the eighteenth-century origins of judicial review in the American constitutional system; in order to do so, they had to reconsider the relationship of constitutional limitations under the American system with more traditional European conceptions of higher law limitations on government power. For the most recent discussion of this problem, see Raoul Berger, Congress v. The Supreme Court (Cambridge, Mass., 1969).
19. Bailyn, Ideological Origins, 31; Wood, Creation of the Republic, 259-305.
20. Dargo: New York, 1974; Reid: University Park, Pa., 1977, 1979; Wroth and Zobel: Cambridge, Mass., 1965.
21. Nelson: Cambridge, Mass., 1975; Horwitz: Cambridge, Mass., 1977.
22. See Nelson, Americanization, 54-63, 136-44; Horwitz, Transformation, 160-73.
23. Paul Boyer and Stephen Nissenbaum, Salem Village Witchcraft (Belmont, Calif., 1973), 183-98, 240-312. See also Boyer and Nissenbaum, Salem Possessed (Cambridge, Mass., 1974), 45-58, 61-79.
24. David Thomas Konig, ed., Plymouth Court Records, 1686-1859 (Wilmington, Del., 1978), entries for Mar. 1743/44, Mar. 1745/46, Dec. 1756, Oct. 1769: II, 222, 238; III, 85, 282.
25. Ibid., III, 282-83.
26. Lovejoy: New York, 1972.

27. Wood, *Creation of the Republic*, 306-564.

Marc Egnal (Pages 43-60)

1. *Faction* and *party* are used in this paper in their eighteenth-century sense—a group of men who worked together on one or more issues—rather than in the modern sense òf a formal political structure. The rudiments of a consciously designed organization were present, however, in Pennsylvania from the 1740's onward and in New York and Massachusetts at the end of the colonial period.

2. For example, Everett Kimball, *The Public Life of Joseph Dudley: A Study of the Colonial Policy of the Stuarts in New England, 1660-1715* (London, 1911); John A. Schutz, *William Shirley: King's Governor of Massachusetts* (Chapel Hill, N.C., 1961).

3. For example, Bernard Bailyn, *The Origins of American Politics* (New York, 1968); Jack P. Greene, *The Quest for Power: The Lower Houses of Assembly in the Southern Royal Colonies, 1689-1776* (Chapel Hill, N.C., 1963).

4. One exception is Stephen E. Patterson, *Political Parties in Revolutionary Massachusetts* (Madison, Wis., 1973).

5. On the colonial economy, see United States Bureau of the Census, *Historical Statistics of the United States, Colonial Times to 1957* (Washington, 1960), 756-57; Michael Kammen, *Colonial New York: A History* (New York, 1975), 91, 161-90; Marc Egnal, "The Economic Development of the Thirteen Continental Colonies, 1720 to 1775," *William and Mary Quarterly*, 3rd ser., 32 (1975), 191-222.

6. The single most useful source on factional conflicts in early Pennsylvania is Gary B. Nash, *Quakers and Politics: Pennsylvania, 1681-1726* (Princeton, N.J., 1968).

7. Nash, *Quakers and Politics*, 16-318; "An Early Petition of the Freemen of the Province of Pennsylvania to the Assembly, 1692," *Pennsylvania Magazine of History and Biography* (hereafter cited as *PMHB*), 38 (1914), 495-501; James Logan to William Penn, Sept. 25, 1700, *PMHB*, 43 (1918), 86-88.

8. Thomas Wendel, "The Keith-Lloyd Alliance: Factional and Coalition Politics in Colonial Pennsylvania," *PMHB*, 92 (1968), 289-305; P. Keith, *Chronicles of Pennsylvania from the English Revolution* . . . (1917; reprinted Port Washington, N.Y., 1969), III, 666-715; Richard Lester, "Currency Issues to Overcome Depressions in Pennsylvania, 1723 to 1729," in Ralph Andreano, ed., *New Views on American Economic Development* (Cambridge, Mass., 1965), 73-97.

9. Lester, "Currency Issues," 106-12; Keith, *Chronicles of Pennsylvania*, III, 711-25. Leonard W. Labaree et al., eds., *The Autobiography of Benjamin Franklin* (New Haven, 1964), 124-25, presents a different perspective on the 1729 currency issue.

10. Jerome R. Reich, *Leisler's Rebellion: A Study of Democracy in New York, 1664-1720* (Chicago, 1953), 55-126; Irving Mark, *Agrarian Conflicts in Colonial New York, 1711-1775*, 2nd ed. (Port Washington, N.Y., 1965), 19-28; William Smith, Jr., *The History of the Province of New York*, Michael Kammen, ed. (Cambridge, Mass., 1972), I, 70-75; Lawrence H. Leder, *Robert Livingston, 1654-1728, and the Politics of Colonial New York*

(Chapel Hill, N.C., 1961), 61-64; Patricia U. Bonomi, *A Factious People: Politics and Society in Colonial New York* (New York, 1971), 75-76.

11. Cited in Mark, *Agrarian Conflicts,* 25-26; Leder, *Livingston,* 87-95, 120-22, 129-60; Smith, *History,* I, 92-93, 103-10; Sung Bok Kim, "A New Look at the Great Landlords of Eighteenth-Century New York," *William and Mary Quarterly,* 3rd ser., 27 (1970), 585-86.

12. Leder, *Livingston,* 161-250; Smith, *History,* I, 110-57; Kim, "Great Landlords," 586.

13. Leder, *Livingston,* 250-90; Smith, *History,* I, 166-89; Cadwallader Colden to James Alexander, May 17, June 21, June 30, Nov. 19, 1728, Robert Hunter to James Alexander, Aug. 10, 1728, James Alexander to John Montgomerie, Sept. 4, 1728, James Alexander: A Letter from a Gentleman in New York to his Friend in the Country, Oct. 22, 1728, Lewis Morris, Jr. to James Alexander, Oct. 22, 1728, Jan. 1729, Rutherfurd Collection, I, 49, 53, 55, 59, 73, 95, 105, New-York Historical Society (N-YHS); James Alexander to Cadwallader Colden, Dec. 5, 1751, *New-York Historical Society Collections,* 53 (1920), 303-4; Cadwallader Colden to Alexander Colden, Jan. 31, 1760, Smith, *History,* I, 318.

14. Smith, *History,* II, 3-23; Philip Livingston to James Alexander, Jan. 7, Oct. 11, 15, 1735, James Alexander to Lewis Morris, June 16, Nov. 6, 1735, Rutherfurd Collection, II, 97, 103, 137, 139, 143, N-YHS.

15. John Kinsey to Alexander, Smith, Ashfield, and Morris, May 16, 1735, "Names of those agreeing to sustain Col. Morris," c. 1734, Rutherfurd Collection, II, 75, 119, N-YHS.

16. For factional divisions, see the four votes on salaries, Oct. 13, 1738, and the vote on erecting a fort, Sept. 20, 1739, *Journal of the Votes and Proceedings of the General Assembly of the Colony of New York, 1691-1765* (New York, 1764-65), II; Philip Livingston to Robert Livingston, Jr., Mar. 24, 1739, Livingston Family Papers, reel 7, Franklin D. Roosevelt Library.

17. Thomas Hutchinson, *The History of the Colony and Province of Massachusetts-Bay,* Lawrence Mayo, ed. (Cambridge, Mass., 1936), II, 121-25; Richard S. Dunn, *Puritans and Yankees: The Winthrop Dynasty of New England, 1630-1717* (Princeton, N.J., 1962), 258-85. A valuable source for an analysis of factions is William H. Whitmore, *The Massachusetts Civil List for the Colonial and Provincial Periods, 1630-1774* (Albany, 1870).

18. Hutchinson, *History,* II, 117-21; Cotton Mather to John Barnard, July 1, 1707, to Stephen Sewall, Dec. 13, 1707, to John Maxwell of Pollock, Aug. 12, 1712, Kenneth Silverman, ed., *Selected Letters of Cotton Mather* (Baton Rouge, La., 1971), 73, 75, 104, and see 23, 55-61; diary entries of May 31, 1705, Apr. 11, 1707, M. Halsey Thomas, ed., *The Diary of Samuel Sewall, 1674-1729* (New York, 1973), I, 524, 564.

19. Hutchinson, *History,* II, 96-113.

20. *Ibid.,* II, 155-56.

21. *Ibid.,* II, 157-59; Cotton Mather to Sir William Ashurst, Oct. 12, 1714, *Selected Letters,* 153-45, and see 141-43.

22. Hutchinson, *History,* II, 163-249; Cotton Mather to William Ashurst, Dec. 10, 1717, to Increase Mather, c. Feb. 1718, to Jeremiah Dummer, Jan. 19, 1719, to Robert Wodrow, Jan. 1, 1723, June 15, 1725, *Selected Letters,* 244, 252-53, 271-72, 356-57, 407.

23. Hutchinson, *History,* II, 243.

24. William Douglass to Cadwallader Colden, Nov. 20, 1727, *N-YHS Collections*, 50 (1977), 238.
25. Hutchinson, *History*, II, 255-87, quote on 284; William Douglass to Cadwallader Colden, Apr. 22, Sept. 9, 1728, *N-YHS Collections*, 50 (1917), 257-58, 270.
26. Hutchinson, *History*, II, 298-304.
27. Benjamin Franklin, "A Plan for Settling Two Western Colonies," 1754, Leonard W. Labaree et al., eds., *The Papers of Benjamin Franklin* (New Haven, 1959—), V, 456-63, quote on 457; Benjamin Franklin to Peter Collinson, May 28, 1754, *ibid.*, V, 332.
28. Among the documents used for delineating factional lines are "Dancing Academy," 1748, Thomas J. Scharf and Thompson Westcott, *History of Philadelphia: 1609-1884* (Philadelphia, 1884), II, 864; Association Militia, *Pennsylvania Gazette*, Jan. 5, 1748; Protest against Quaker Assembly, 1755, *PMHB*, 10 (1886), 296-97; Petition for Royal Government, 1764, Privy Council, bundle 50, Public Record Office (PRO), London; Petition against Royal Government, Sept., 1764, Epistles Received, London Yearly Meeting, Friends House Library, London; Common Councilmen, *Pennsylvania Archives* (Philadelphia, Harrisburg, 1852-1935), 2nd ser., IX, 751-52; Justices of the Peace, *Pennsylvania Archives*, 2nd ser., IX, 700-13; Vestrymen of Christ Church, Philadelphia, *PMHB*, 19 (1895), 518-26; Presbyterians, Scharf and Westcott, *Philadelphia*, II, 1267.
29. George Thomas to Board of Trade, Oct. 20, 1740, CO5/1233/192-201, PRO; Directors of Library Company to Proprietors, July 1742, *Franklin Papers*, II, 348.
30. Edwin B. Bronner, "The Disgrace of John Kinsey, Quaker Politician, 1739-1750," *PMHB*, 75 (1951), 400-15; Frederick B. Tolles, *Meeting House and Counting House: The Quaker Merchants of Colonial Philadelphia, 1682-1763* (Chapel Hill, N.C., 1948), 23-24.
31. Benjamin Franklin to Cadwallader Colden, Nov. 27, 1747, Richard Peters to Proprietors, Nov. 29, 1747, *Franklin Papers*, III, 213, 215-17; *Pennsylvania Gazette*, Jan. 5, 1748; John Smith to Elizabeth Hudson, Oct. 10, 1750, John Smith Correspondence, Historical Society of Pennsylvania (HSP).
32. Marc Egnal, "The Politics of Ambition: A New Look at Benjamin Franklin's Career," *Canadian Review of American Studies*, 6 (1975), 153-55. For an examination of these events from the point of view of two expansionists, see Willing Letterbook and Kidd Letterbook, HSP.
33. Richard Peters to Thomas Penn, June 1, 1756, Benjamin Franklin to Peter Collinson, June 15, 1756, *Franklin Papers*, VI, 457n, 456-57; *ibid.*, VII, 10n; William Logan to John Smith, Oct. 1, 1756, John Smith Correspondence, HSP.
34. Egnal, "Politics of Ambition," 151-64.
35. Daniel Roberdeau to John Boyd, Jan. 17, 1766, to William Turnbull, Nov. 25, 1766, Nov. 11, 1768, Roberdeau Letterbook, HSP; Charles Thomson to Cooke, Lawrence, & Co., Nov. 9, 1765, *N-YHS Collections*, II (1878), 8-11.
36. John Reynell to James Shirley, May 14, 1765, Reynell Letterbook, HSP; John Drinker and Stephen Collins to Israel Pemberton, Sept. 25, 1766, Pemberton Papers, HSP. James Hutson, *Pennsylvania Politics, 1746-1770: The Movement for Royal Government and Its Consequences* (Princeton, N.J., 1972), 210-39, argues that the Presbyterians formed a separate faction.

37. Stamp Act Remonstrance, Scharf and Westcott, *Philadelphia,* I, 272-73; John Reynell to Andreas Groth, May 11, 1768, Reynell Letterbook, HSP; Townshend Act Remonstrance, Samuel Hazard, ed., *Hazard's Register of Pennsylvania . . .* (Philadelphia, 1828-35), II, 222-24; Thomas Clifford to Walter Franklin, Mar. 11, 1769, Clifford Letterbook, HSP; Israel Pemberton to John Pemberton, July 24, 1769, Pemberton Papers, HSP; *Pennsylvania Gazette,* May 10, 1770.

38. Diary entries of Aug. 30, 31, Sept. 1, 11, 1774, Sept. 16, 1775, L.H. Butterfield, ed., *Diary and Autobiography of John Adams* (New York, 1964), II, 115, 117, 119, 132, 173; R.A. Ryerson, "Political Mobilization and the American Revolution: The Resistance Movement in Philadelphia, 1765 to 1776," *William and Mary Quarterly,* 3rd ser., 31 (1974), 565-88; Merrill Jensen,*Founding of a Nation: A History of the American Revolution, 1763-1776* (New York, 1968), 525-28, 596-98, 641-42, 656, 681-88.

39. Two incisive surveys of factional conflict are Bonomi, *Factious People,* and Stanley N. Katz, *Newcastle's New York: Anglo-American Politics, 1732-1753* (Cambridge, Mass., 1968). Also of first importance in delineating New York's factions are the hundreds of votes recorded in *New York Assembly Journals, 1691-1765* and *Journals of the Votes and Proceedings of the General Assembly of the Colony of New York, from 1766 to 1776 inclusive* (Albany, 1820).

40. Smith, *History,* II, 46-61; Nicholas Varga, "New York Government and Politics During the Mid-Eighteenth Century" (unpublished Ph.D. diss., Fordham University, 1960), 65-73, 227-28, 282-83, 340; Philip Livingston to Robert Livingston, Jr., Mar. 13, 1745, Livingston Family Papers, reel 7, FDR Library.

41. Smith, *History,* II, 68-105; Varga, "New York Government," 84-122, 232-33, 360-64; Cadwallader Colden to Duke of Newcastle, Mar. 21, 1748, *N-YHS Collections,* 53 (1920), 22.

42. Varga, "New York Government," 122; Bonomi, *Factious People,* 153-58; George Clinton to Cadwallader Colden, June 30, Sept. 7, 1748, *N-YHS Collections,* 53 (1920), 69, 76.

43. Smith, *History,* II, 97; Varga, "New York Government," 125-26. For the division over defense spending, see the following votes: July 4, Aug. 21, Dec. 24, 1745, Jan. 18, 28, Feb. 5, 13, Apr. 7, 9 (4 votes), 23, 24, June 4, 1746, *New York Assembly Journals, 1691-1765,* II.

44. Smith, *History,* II, 97, 113-38; Varga, "New York Government," 152-81; George Clinton to Cadwallader Colden, Feb. 9, 1750, James Alexander to Cadwallader Colden, Dec. 5, 1751, *N-YHS Collections,* 53 (1920), 189, 303; Robert R. Livingston to Robert Livingston, Jr., July 23, 1750, Robert R. Livingston Collection, Box 1, N-YHS; John Livingston to Robert Livingston, Jr., Nov. 5, 1751, Mar. 25, 1752, Philip Livingston II to Robert Livingston, Jr., Feb. 15, 1752, Livingston Family Papers, reel 7, FDR Library; Cadwallader Colden to James Alexander, June 3, 1751, Rutherfurd Collection, IV, 81, N-YHS.

45. Smith, *History,* II, 142-45, 166-68, 201, 207-8; Varga, "New York Government," 200-3; William Livingston to Robert Livingston, Jr., Feb. 4, 1754, John Van Der Spiegel to Robert Livingston, Jr., June 19, 1755, Livingston Family Papers, reel 7, FDR Library. See also the following votes: Nov. 26, 28 (3 votes), 1754, June 12, 1755, *New York Assembly Journals, 1691-1765, II.*

46. Smith, *History,* II, 150-55, 162-63, 179-247; William Pepperell to Peter,

John, and Philip Livingston, and unknown, Mar. 25, 1755, William Shirley to John Erving, William Alexander, and Lewis Morris, Jr., Apr. 24, 1755, Rutherfurd Collection, III, 57, 55, N-YHS; William Shirley to William Johnson, May 7, 1755, to James DeLancey, June 1, 1755, Charles H. Lincoln, ed., *Correspondence of William Shirley, Governor of Massachusetts and Military Commander in America, 1731-1760* (1912; reprinted New York, 1973), II, 167-68, 184-85; also *ibid.,* II, 216n.

47. Varga, "New York Government," 248n. See the following votes: Mar. 21, 22, 1760, *New York Assembly Journals, 1691-1765,* II.

48. William Smith, *Historical Memoirs of William Smith,* William H. W. Sabine, ed. (New York, 1956), I, 32-33, 47-49; Robert R. Livingston to unknown, Nov. 2, 1765, Livingston Papers, Bancroft Transcripts, New York Public Library; Colden's Declaration about Stamped Paper, Nov. 2-4, 1765, Robert R. Livingston to Robert Monckton, Jan. 23, 1768, John Watts to Robert Monckton, Jan. 23, 1768, *Massachusetts Historical Society Collections,* 4th ser., 10 (1871), 581-82, 560, 599.

49. Robert R. Livingston to Robert Livingston, Jr., Feb. 18, 1766, Robert R. Livingston Collection, Box 1, N-YHS; Robert R. Livingston to John Sargent, May 2, 1766, Livingston Papers, Bancroft Transcripts, NYPL; Robert R. Livingston to Robert Livingston, Jr., May 14, 1766, Livingston Family Papers, reel 8, FDR Library. See the vote of Dec. 12, 1766, *New York Assembly Journals, 1766-1776.*

50. Bonomi, *Factious People,* 267-78; Carl L. Becker, *The History of Political Parties in the Province of New York, 1760-1776* (1909; reprinted Madison, Wis., 1968), 95-276; Smith, *Memoirs,* I, 60-68; Peter R. Livingston to Robert Livingston, Jr., Apr. 24, 1769, James Duane to Robert Livingston, Jr., June 14, 1769, June 7, 1775, Livingston Family Papers, reel 8, FDR Library; diary entries of Aug. 20, 21, 22, 1774, *Diary and Autobiography of John Adams,* II, 102-8.

51. Of particular value in determining party lines are Patterson, *Political Parties;* Schutz, *William Shirley:* Whitmore, *Massachusetts Civil List;* the votes in *Journals of the House of Representatives of Massachusetts* (Boston, 1916-   );list of "land bankers," 1740, *Colonial Society of Massachusetts Publications,* 4 (1910), 166-94; list of "silver bankers," 1740, *ibid.,* 4, 195-200; and hard-money advocates, c. 1748, *Connecticut Historical Society Collections,* 15 (1914), 183-86.

52. Schutz, *Shirley,* 50-62, 71, 83-85, 107; John J. Waters, Jr., *The Otis Family in Provincial and Revolutionary Massachusetts* (Chapel Hill, N.C., 1968), 89-97; Robert Zemsky, *Merchants, Farmers, and River Gods: An Essay on Eighteenth-Century American Politics* (Boston, 1971), 118-21.

53. Hutchinson, *History,* II, 306-8; Schutz, *Shirley,* 92; Zemsky, *Merchants, Farmers, and River Gods,* 118-21; William Shirley to Duke of Newcastle, Oct. 17, 1741, Jan. 23, 1742, *Shirley Correspondence,* I, 79, 80.

54. Hutchinson, *History,* II, 329-30n; Robert J. Taylor, *Western Massachusetts in the Revolution* (Providence, 1954), chaps. 1-5; John Stoddard to William Shirley, Apr. 24, 1745, William Shirley to John Stoddard, Apr. 10, 1747, *Shirley Correspondence,* I, 209-10, 383.

55. Hutchinson, *History,* II, 309-15, III, 255; Schutz, *Shirley,* 70.

56. Hutchinson, *History,* II, 333-37, III, 6-7; Schutz, *Shirley,* 122-28, 143-46; Thomas Hutchinson to [Israel Williams?], Feb. 1, 1748, Israel Williams Papers, Massachusetts Historical Society (MHS); William Shirley to Duke of Bedford, Jan. 31, 1749, *Shirley Correspondence,* I, 462.

57. Hutchinson, *History*, III, 12-13; Schutz, *Shirley*, 137, 142-50, 242n.
58. Schutz, *Shirley*, 176-79m 188, 198. See also the following votes: Jan. 3, Apr. 22, Dec. 14, 27, 1754, June 26, 1755, *Journals of the Massachusetts House of Representatives*, XXX, XXXI, XXXII.
59. Hutchinson, *History*, III, 41-42; Patterson, *Political Parties*, 50-52; Waters, *Otis Family*, 100-07, 116-17. See also the following votes: Oct. 12, 1758, Oct. 9, 1759, *Journals of the House of Representatives*, XXXV, XXXVI.
60. Thomas Hutchinson to Israel Williams, July 30, 1758, see also same to same, Jan. 26, 1754, July 17, 1758, Apr. 24, 1759, Mar. 25, Aug. 25, 1760, Israel Williams Papers, MHS; Hutchinson, *History*, III, 18-20, 28, 34-35; Zemsky, *Merchants, Farmers, and River Gods*, 44-45.
61. William Shirley to Israel Williams, Sept. 26, 1754, Oliver Partridge to Israel Williams, Feb. 11, 1755, Justices of Hampshire to Thomas Pownall, May 19, 1759, Israel Williams Papers, MHS.
62. Francis Bernard to Thomas Pownall, Aug. 28, 1761, cited in Waters, *Otis Family*, 139; Francis Bernard to Lord Barrington, Apr. 19, Aug. 7, 1760, Edward Channing and Archibald Cary Coolidge, eds., *Barrington-Bernard Correspondence and Illustrative Matter, 1760-1770* (1912; reprinted New York, 1970), 11-12, 15; Hutchinson, *History*, III, 65-70.
63. Thomas Hutchinson to Israel Williams, Aug. 25, 1760, Nov. 17, 1763, Israel Williams Papers, MHS; Francis Bernard to Lord Barrington, May 1, 1762, *Barrington-Bernard Correspondence*, 52-53; Whitmore, *Massachusetts Civil List*.
64. Hutchinson, *History*, III, 113, 145-56; diary entries of Feb. 1763, Dec. 23, 1765, *Diary and Autobiography of John Adams*, I, 238, 270-71; Francis Bernard to Lord Barrington, July 30, 1768, *Barrington-Bernard Correspondence*, 169-70.
65. Thomas Hutchinson to Israel Williams, Apr. 15, 1763, Israel Williams Papers, MHS; Taylor, *Western Massachusetts*, chap. 4. See the following votes: Feb. 1, 1764 (2 votes), Feb. 1, 1765, June 30, 1768, *Journals of the Massachusetts House of Representatives*, XL, XLI, XLV.
66. Hutchinson, *History*, III, 99-100, 117-18, 185; Report of Committee of Merchants and accompanying lists of signers of non-importation agreement, Mar. 1768, Samuel Philips Savage Papers, Thomas Cushing to Dennys DeBerdt, Apr. 18, 1768: Miscellaneous Bound, Subscribers to Non-Importation, Large Collection, MHS.
67. Hutchinson, *History*, 248-51, 255-60; Richard D. Brown, *Revolutionary Politics in Massachusetts; The Boston Committee of Correspondence and the Towns, 1772-1774* (1970; reprinted New York, 1976), 59-60; Thomas Hutchinson to Israel Williams, Dec. 10, 1770, Jan. 10, 23, Apr. 1, 1771, Israel Williams Papers, MHS; diary entries of Feb. 14, May 22, June 13, 1771, Dec. 24, 31, 1772, *Diary and Autobiography of John Adams*, II, 5, 15, 34-35, 49-50, 72, 75.
68. Thomas Hutchinson to Israel Williams, May 14, 1774, Israel Williams Papers, MHS; James H. Stark, *The Loyalists of Massachusetts and the Other Side of the American Revolution* (Boston, 1910), 124-40; Marc Egnal, "Society and Politics in Massachusetts, 1774 to 1778" (M.A. thesis, University of Wisconsin, 1967).
69. Marc Egnal and Joseph A. Ernst, "An Economic Interpretation of the American Revolution," *William and Mary Quarterly*, 3rd ser., 29 (1972), 3-32.

Alison Gilbert Olson (Pages 61-69)

1. Historians of party seem to have been hung up on the attempt to establish a "true" definition of party, and Egnal himself refers at times to parties, factions, and groups. In twentieth-century terms, factions are generally seen as an enduring form of coalition, while parties involve a higher degree of organization than factions and greater appeal to constituents. Do we take this twentieth-century distinction (or whatever twentieth-century definitions we like) and extend it back to the eighteenth century, or can we be more flexible in our definition and apply the label *party* to more primitive organizations in a line of evolution? How primitive can a partisan group be and still deserve to be called a party? We are determined that there must be a "right" answer. But since *party, faction, group,* etc. are simply labels, the "right" one must be one that most historians accept as useful. To the extent that divisions over the question of expansion provide the most consistent explanation for political divisions within the colonies after 1740, we can usefully label them as the source of parties.

2. See the same argument made against British acquisition of Bengal by Sir William Meredith, May 10, 1773, in T.C. Hansard, *Parliamentary History of England* (London, 1813), XVII, 857.

3. Major L. Wilson, *Space, Time, and Freedom* (Westport, Conn., 1975), chap. III.

4. Alison Gilbert Olson, "1776: the Revolution Against Parliament," paper delivered at Folger Library Conference, Washington, May 21-22, 1976.

5. *Gentleman's Magazine,* 24 (1754), 504.

6. Quoted in Klaus E. Knorr, *British Colonial Theories, 1570-1850* (Toronto, 1944), 106.

7. Newcastle to Murray, Sept. 10, 1754, British Museum, Add. ms. 32,736, pp. 472-74.

8. For British doubts about war with the French, see Stanley M. Pargellis, *Lord Loudon in North America* (New Haven, 1933), 1-30; John Shebbeare, *A Fourth Letter to the People of England* (London, 1756), 7.

9. On this point, see especially the Introduction to Geoffrey Symcox, *War, Diplomacy, and Imperialism 1618-1763* (New York, 1973); Max Savelle, "The American Balance of Power and European Diplomacy, 1713-78," in Richard B. Morris, ed., *The Era of the American Revolution* (New York, 1939).

10. Jack Sosin, *Whitehall and the Wilderness* (Lincoln, Nebr., 1961), esp. 4, 117, 151, 238.

11. The variety of the interest groups concerned in the frontier is suggested in Jack Sosin, *The Revolutionary Frontier, 1763-1783* (New York, 1967), 32.

12. Duverger emphasizes common local interests, ideology, and shared political ambitions in the creation of these "parliamentary groups." *Political Parties, Their Organization and Activity in the Modern State,* rev. 2nd ed. (London, 1959), xxiii-xxv.

David R. Chesnutt (Pages 70-86)

1. William Drayton to James Grant, Oct. 29, 1768, "Papers of General

James Grant of Ballindalloch, sometime Governor of East Florida, in ownership of Sir Ewan Macpherson-Grant, Bart. [Requests for access through 'The Secretary, National Register of Archives (Scotland), P.O. Box 36, Edinburgh']" (Ballindalloch Castle Muniments).

2. Robert M. Weir, " 'The Harmony We Were Famous For': An Interpretation of Pre-Revolutionary South Carolina Politics," *William and Mary Quarterly,* 3rd ser., 21 (1964), 479-89; Eugene Sirmans, *Colonial South Carolina: A Political History, 1663-1763* (Chapel Hill, N.C., 1966), 164-67, 311-13, 314; Jack P. Greene, *The Quest for Power: The Lower Houses of Assembly in the Southern Royal Colonies, 1689-1776* (Chapel Hill, N.C., 1963), 191-96, 252, 357-60, 403-16; David R. Chesnutt, "South Carolina's Expansion into Colonial Georgia, 1720-1765" (Ph.D. diss., University of Georgia, 1973), 202-10; Philip M. Hamer et al., eds., *The Papers of Henry Laurens* (Columbia, S.C., 1968-   ), IV, 117-18, 431, 451-52, 456-57, 529-30; James Glen to Duke of Newcastle, Feb. 6, 1743/44, *Collections of the South-Carolina Historical Society,* 2 (1858), 286.

3. Richard Maxwell Brown, *The South Carolina Regulators* (Cambridge, Mass., 1963), 38-40, 42, 43, 115.

4. Extensive treatment of the Circuit Court Act of 1768 is given in Brown, *South Carolina Regulators,* 64-76. Leaders in both sections realized the act was in jeopardy. Committee of Correspondence to Charles Garth, Apr. 15, 1768, Garth Letterbook, South Carolina Archives; Edward McCrady, *The History of South Carolina under the Royal Government, 1719-1776* (New York, 1899), 640.

5. Brown, *South Carolina Regulators,* 53-58; *South Carolina & American General Gazette,* Aug. 5, 19, 26, Sept. 2, 9, 1768; William Bull to Earl of Hillsborough, July 18, Sept. 10, 1768, Sainsbury Transcripts of Records in the British Public Record Office relating to South Carolina (BPRO Trans.), XXXII (1768-70), 14-16, 37-41, S.C. Archives.

6. The three backcountry parishes were St. Mark (1757), St. Matthew (1768), and St. David (1768). Thomas Cooper and David J. McCord, eds., *The Statutes at Large of South Carolina* (Columbia, S.C., 1837-41), IV, 35-37, 298-302. Commons House Journals, XXXVII, part 2, 49, XXXVIII, part 1, 69, 72, 75-76, 86, S.C. Archives; Peter Timothy to Benjamin Franklin, Sept. 3, 1768, Leonard W. Labaree et al., eds., *The Papers of Benjamin Franklin* (New Haven, 1959-   ), XV, 199-203, quote on 202.

7. *South-Carolina Gazette,* Aug. 8, Sept. 12, 1768; William Bull to Earl of Hillsborough, Sept. 10, 1768, BPRO Trans., XXXII, 39-40, S.C. Archives.

8. *S.C. Gazette,* Oct. 10, 1768; House Journals, XXXVII, part 2, 2-4, 7-8, S.C. Archives; Brown, *South Carolina Regulators,* 61-62.

9. *South Carolina Historical Magazine (SCHM),* 29 (1928), 76; Brown, *South Carolina Regulators,* 104; House Journals, XXXVII, part 2, 7, XXXVIII, part 1, 69, 72, 75-76, 86, S.C. Archives. The planters returned for St. Paul were Benjamin and Charles Elliott and Archibald Stanyarne. St. Bartholomew returned James Parsons, James Reid, James Skirving, Jr., and Rawlins Lowndes. *S.C. Gazette,* Oct. 10, 1768.

10. *S.C. Gazette,* Oct. 3, 1768.

11. For the exchange of letters between the house speakers of Massachusetts, Virginia, and South Carolina, see House Journals, XXXVII, part 2, 9-16, S.C. Archives. Peter Manigault's letter of July 30, 1768, to Massachusetts Speaker Thomas Cushing was published in the *S.C.*

Gazette, Sept. 12, 1768, under a Boston dateline of Aug. 13, 1768.

12. Hiller B. Zobel, *The Boston Massacre* (New York, 1970), 69, 82.

13. *S.C. General Gazette*, Sept. 16, 23, 1768; William Bull to Earl of Hillsborough, Oct. 18, 1768, BPRO Trans., XXXII, 56, S.C. Archives.

14. Joseph A. Ernst, *Money and Politics in America, 1755-1775: A Study in the Currency Act of 1764 and the Political Economy of Revolution* (Chapel Hill, N.C., 1973), 215-18.

15. Richard Walsh stresses the inactivity of the merchants rather than the internal problems posed by the Regulators. Richard Walsh, *Charleston's Sons of Liberty: A Study of the Artisans, 1763-1789* (Columbia, S.C., 1959), 45.

16. Transcripts of the Manuscript Books and Papers of the Commission of Enquiry into Losses and Services of the American Loyalists preserved amongst the Audit Office Records in the Public Record Office of England, 1783-90, made for the New York Public Library, LIV, 19-22; *SCHM*, 7 (1906), 29; *ibid*, 20 (1919), 19; Henry Laurens to James Grant, Feb. 11, 1762, Ballindalloch Castle Muniments; Greene, *Quest for Power*, 484.

17. *S.C. Gazette*, Oct. 3, 1768.

18. Laurens and Pinckney were among the ten leading members of the Commons House in the 1760's. Greene, *Quest for Power*, 481, 484; Jack P. Greene, ed., *The Nature of Colony Constitutions; Two Pamphlets on the Wilkes Fund Controversy in South Carolina By Sir Egerton Leigh and Arthur Lee* (Columbia, S.C., 1970), 9.

19. *S.C. Gazette*, Oct. 3, 1768; Henry Laurens to James Grant, Oct. 1, 1768, Ballindalloch Castle Muniments.

20. *S.C. General Gazette*, Oct. 7, 1768; Henry Laurens to James Grant, Dec. 22, 1768, Ballindalloch Castle Muniments.

21. *Papers of Henry Laurens*, III, 270-72, 324, 352, IV, 165, 286; Leila Sellers, *Charleston Business on the Eve of the American Revolution* (Chapel Hill, N.C., 1934), 185-89, 205-8, 222-26; Walsh, *Charleston's Sons of Liberty*, 35-38, 46-48, 60-63; George C. Rogers, Jr., "The Charleston Tea Party: The Significance of December 3, 1773," *SCHM*, 75 (1974), 160-61.

22. William Bull to Earl of Hillsborough, Oct. 18, 23, 1768, BPRO Trans., XXXII, 56-57, 89, S.C. Archives.

23. Henry Laurens to James Habersham, Nov. 17, 1768, Laurens Papers, South Carolina Historical Society.

24. House Journals, XXXVII, part 2, 2-9, S.C. Archives.

25. William Wragg, "To The Electors of St. John's Parish, Colleton County," Sept. 15, Oct. 7, 1768, *S.C. General Gazette*, Sept. 16, Oct. 7, 1768; John Mackenzie, "To Every Freeholder In The Province," Sept. 26, 1768, *S.C. Gazette*, Sept. 26, 1768.

26. Journal, Court of Common Pleas, 1763-69, 173, 176, 177, 181-92, S.C. Archives; Robert M. Weir, "Liberty and Property and No Stamps; South Carolina During the Stamp Act Crisis" (Ph.D. diss., Western Reserve University, 1966), 390, 395-96; William Bull to Earl of Hillsborough, Dec. 5, 1770, K.G. Davies, ed., *Documents of the American Revolution, 1770-1783: Colonial Office Series* (Shannon, Ire., 1972-   ), II, 284.

27. Robert M. Weir, "The South Carolinian as Extremist," *South Atlantic Quarterly*, 74 (1975), 89-90.

28. House Journals, XXXVII, part 2, 9-21, S.C. Archives; Charles Montagu to Earl of Hillsborough, Nov. 21, 1768, BPRO Trans., XXXII, 61, S.C. Archives; *S.C. Gazette*, Nov. 21, 1768.

29. William Bull to Earl of Hillsborough, Sept. 10, 1768, BPRO Trans., XXX-II, 40, S.C. Archives. A writer signing himself "Rusticus" challenged the ability of the Regulators' leaders to deal effectively with the constitutional issues which would face the forthcoming assembly. *S.C. Gazette,* Oct. 3, 1768. The importance of unified resistance is discussed by Richard Buel, Jr., "Democracy and the American Revolution: A Frame of Reference," *William and Mary Quarterly,* 3rd ser., 21 (1964), 174-75. Greene suggests the same spirit of one-upmanship in his discussion of the Wilkes Fund controversy in *Nature of Colony Constitutions,* 7.

30. Brown, *South Carolina Regulators,* 83-85, 97-102; Richard J. Hooker, ed., *The Carolina Backcountry on the Eve of the Revolution: the Journal and Other Writings of Charles Woodmason, Anglican Itinerant* (Chapel Hill, N.C., 1953), 207, 242, 267; St. Mark returned Joseph Kershaw; St. David, George Gabriel Powell; St. Matthew, William Thompson; Prince William, Patrick Calhoun; and St. Stephen, Tacitus Gaillard. House Journals, XX-XVIII, part 1, 13, 49, S.C. Archives. For the maneuvers over nonimportation, see Walsh, *Charleston's Sons of Liberty,* 46-49; Sellers, *Charleston Business,* 203-20.

31. Brown, *South Carolina Regulators,* 97-102, 148-58.

32. House Journals, XXXVIII, part 1, 13, 69, 72, 75-76, 86, 107, 115, S.C. Archives.

33. Benjamin Smith to William Smith, May 16, 1766, quoted in George C. Rogers, Jr., *Evolution of a Federalist: William Loughton Smith of Charleston, 1759-1812* (Columbia, S.C., 1959), 47. For Gadsden and the mechanics' meeting, see R.W. Gibbes, ed., *Documentary History of the American Revolution, 1764-1776* (New York, 1855), I, 10-11.

34. Walsh, *Charleston's Sons of Liberty,* 45-50; Pauline Maier views the General Committee as part of a developing pattern which culminated in September 1769 with a General Meeting of the Inhabitants which became "a surrogate for the New England town meeting." Pauline Maier, *From Resistance to Revolution: Colonial Radicals and the Development of American Opposition to Britain, 1765-1776* (New York, 1972), 118.

Joseph A. Ernst (Pages 87-97)

1. The following is based upon Joseph A. Ernst, "Growth of the Commons House of Assembly of South Carolina, 1761-1775" (unpublished M.A. thesis, University of Wisconsin, 1958), and a forthcoming study, "The Political Economy of the American Revolution: The Southern Colonies."

2. The letter, written on Dec. 13, 1762, appeared in Wells' *Weekly Gazette* on Jan. 5, 1763. This issue of the paper is missing, but the letter was republished in Peter Timothy's *South-Carolina Gazette* on Feb. 5, 1763. The standard work on the Boone affair is Jack P. Greene, "The Gadsden Election Controversy and the Revolutionary Movement in South Carolina," *Mississippi Valley Historical Review,* 46 (1959), 469-92.

3. Gadsden's letter is reprinted in Richard Walsh, ed., *The Writings of Christopher Gadsden, 1764-1805* (Columbia, S.C., 1966), 17-50. Laurens' letter appeared in Wells' *South-Carolina Weekly Gazette* on Mar. 2, 1763. This issue is missing, but Gadsden summarized Laurens' remarks in another letter to the *South-Carolina Gazette* of Mar. 12, 1763; see *Writings of Gadsden,* 54-61.

Concerning the Grant-Middleton dispute and the conflict between Laurens and Gadsden, see Philip M. Hamer et al., eds., *The Papers of Henry Laurens* (Columbia, S.C., 1968-   ), III, 270-71, 275-355; George C. Rogers, Jr., "The Papers of James Grant of Ballindalloch Castle, Scotland," *The South Carolina Historical Magazine,* 77 (1976), 146-49.

4. Jan. 4, 6, 1764, Journals of the Commons House of Assembly of South Carolina, William Sumner Jenkins, ed., *Records of the States of the United States of America: A Microfilm Compilation* (Washington, 1949), hereafter cited as "Journals of S.C. Commons House."

5. Henry Laurens to Christopher Rowe, Feb. 8, 1764, *Papers of Henry Laurens,* IV, 164-65. Laurens had his own investments in trade and land in the backcountry and was an acknowledged "friend" of the "Country People"; see, for instance, *Papers of Henry Laurens,* III, 52, 56; Richard J. Hooker, ed., *The Carolina Backcountry on the Eve of the Revolution: The Journal and Other Writings of Charles Woodmason, Anglican Itinerant* (Chapel Hill, N.C., 1953), 247-52. In contrast, Gadsden, as Laurens points out, had no "stake" in the backcountry and no friendship for the back settlers either; on this last point, see *Papers of Henry Laurens,* III, 353.

6. See, for instance, *South-Carolina Gazette,* Nov. 12, 1764, June 8, 1765, June 2, 1766.

7. The quote is from Jan. 10, 1765, Journals of S.C. Commons House. See also William Bull to the Earl of Halifax, Mar. 1, 1765, and to the Lords of Trade, Mar. 15, Dec. 17, 1765, in Records in the British Public Record Office Relating to South Carolina, 1663-82, XXX, 245-46, 248-51, 300; William Bull's remarks to the council, Oct. 29, 1765, in Journal of the Upper House of Assembly, *Records of the States.*

8. *South-Carolina Gazette,* June 15, 1765.

9. See Ernst, "Commons House of Assembly," 66-70; *Journal of Charles Woodmason,* 167-68, quote on 168.

10. Feb. 27, 1766, Journals of S.C. Commons House.

11. Ernst, "Commons House of Assembly," 73.

12. *Journal of Charles Woodmason,* 10-12, 289, 294.

13. Ernst, "Commons House of Assembly," 74, 76, 77; *Journal of Charles Woodmason,* 289, 292-96, quote on 289. Another instance in which assembly leaders used backcountry grievances to the advantage of the House is the effort to purchase the office of Richard Cumberland, the provincial provost marshal "in abstentia." Space does not permit a discussion of this matter, but see Ernst, "Commons House of Assembly," 74-76.

14. When the term Regulator first made its appearance is a moot question. The important point is that associations of one sort or another for the protection of life and property dated back to at least 1764. See Ernst, "Commons House of Assembly," 74; *South-Carolina Gazette,* Mar. 17, 1767.

15. The quote is from Oct. 5, 1767, Journals of His Majesty's Honorable Council, in *Records of the States.* See also Ernst, "Commons House of Assembly," 77-78. The credit for stopping the march on Charleston seems to have been Bull's; see *Journal of Charles Woodmason,* 191, 204-5.

16. Nov. 5, 1767, Journals of S.C. Commons House.

17. *Journal of Charles Woodmason,* 213-33.

18. See the discussion in Ernst, "Commons House of Assembly," 78-79; the quote is from *Journal of Charles Woodmason,* 205.

19. Ernst, "Commons House of Assembly," 80-81; the quote is from Nov. 10,

1767, Journals of S.C. Commons House.
20. *Journal of Charles Woodmason,* 287. The House journals merely indicate that after a second reading the bill was returned to committee to incorporate minor amendments. But when the bill re-emerged a month later the provision for county courts was missing; see Jan. 20, 1768, Journals of S.C. Commons House.
21. See Apr. 19, 1768, Journals of the Council; Ernst, "Commons House of Assembly," 86-87, 100-02; *Journal of Charles Woodmason,* 175-77.
22. See Ernst, "Commons House of Assembly," 87; *Journal of Charles Woodmason,* 179-84, 206-10, quote on 210.
23. See Ernst, "Commons House of Assembly," 88-90; *Journal of Charles Woodmason,* 90, 211. The pressures on Montagu at this time, according to Woodmason (p. 280), also included an alliance between the Regulators of both the Carolinas and the threat of an armed invasion of South Carolina by the Regulators of North Carolina.
24. Ernst, "Commons House of Assembly," 92-93. See also Joseph A. Ernst, *Money and Politics in America, 1755-1775: A Study in the Currency Act of 1764 and the Political Economy of Revolution* (Chapel Hill, N.C., 1973), 219.
25. *Journal of Charles Woodmason,* 185.
26. Quoted in *Journal of Charles Woodmason,* 189. Some of the long-term effects of this feeling are discussed in Ronald Hoffman, "The 'Disaffected' in the Revolutionary South," in Alfred F. Young, ed., *The American Revolution, Explorations in the History of American Radicalism* (De Kalb, Ill., 1976), 273-316.

George Dargo (Pages 98-114)

1. Patricia U. Bonomi, "The Middle Colonies: Embryo of the New Political Order," in Alden T. Vaughan and George A. Billias, eds., *Perspectives on Early American History* (New York, 1973), 63-92.
2. *Ibid.,* 88
3. Bonomi attributes the subordination of "this emergent tendency" to the requirements of Revolutionary consensus, but my own interpretation, as I explain, is somewhat different. I am, however, following Bonomi's outline on what might loosely be called "the rise and fall" of the notion of party in these times.
4. For example, see Ronald Hoffman, *A Spirit of Dissension: Economics, Politics, and the Revolution in Maryland* (Baltimore, 1973); and Stephen E. Patterson, *Political Parties in Revolutionary Massachusetts* (Madison, Wis., 1973). Patterson has detailed very clearly the sources of "antipartisan theory" in Massachusetts, but the pattern he delineates is quite different from what I have found in Pennsylvania. He suggests that "antipartisan theory" began to collapse under the pressure of "partisan reality" during and after the Revolution, whereas I am proposing that the Revolution reinforced the anti-party theory that had begun to unwind before the Revolution. As Patterson makes clear, traditional, even medieval, values had a special force in New England society, which may well have made political theory in Massachusetts much more resistant to change in the late colonial period. Indeed, the persistence of traditionalism in Massachusetts may have been even greater than Patterson

suggests, for he shows little evidence of "the first substantial adjustments in theory" to partisan reality during and after the Revolution. See Patterson, *Political Parties*, esp. Chaps. 1, 9-10; quote on p. 31.

5. See Lawrence H. Leder, *Liberty and Authority: Early American Political Ideology, 1689-1769* (Chicago, 1968); George Dargo, *Roots of the Republic: A New Perspective on Early American Constitutionalism* (New York, 1974).

6. Hoffman, *Spirit of Dissension*, chap. 8.

7. As I see it, the task of research into the political history of Revolutionary Pennsylvania is to uncover party organization, structure, and method. We know much about the social, economic, and ethnic orientation of politics but little about its actual composition beyond Philadelphia itself.

8. A.H. Smyth, ed., *The Writings of Benjamin Franklin* (New York, 1905-07), X, 120-21; *Pennsylvania Gazette*, May 17, 1786.

9. V.W. Crane, "Franklin's 'The Internal State of America' (1786)," *William and Mary Quarterly*, 3rd ser., 15 (1958), 214-27.

10. Richard Hofstadter, *The Idea of a Party System: The Rise of Legitimate Opposition in the United States, 1780-1840* (Berkeley, Calif., 1969), chap. 6; Michael Wallace, "Changing Concepts of Party in the United States: New York, 1815-1828," *American Historical Review*, 74 (1969), 453-91; Martin Van Buren, *Inquiry into the Origin and Course of Political Parties in the United States* (1867; reprinted New York, 1967), 10-ll, *passim*. But see Ronald P. Formisano, "Deferential-Participant Politics: The Early Republic's Political Culture, 1789-1840," *American Political Science Review*, 68 (1974), 473-87, who puts the reality and acceptance of party even later.

11. *The American Magazine and Monthly Chronicle for the British Colonies*, Vol. 1, no. 1, 34.

12. Bonomi, "The Middle Colonies," esp. 87-92; Bernard Bailyn, *The Origins of American Politics* (New York, 1968), 125-31; Dargo, *Roots of the Republic*, 148-52. For England, see Caroline Robbins, " 'Discordant Parties': A Study of the Acceptance of Party by Englishmen," *Political Science Quarterly*, 73 (1958), 505-29.

13. Seymour Lipset, *The First New Nation: The United States in Historical and Comparative Perspective* (New York, 1963), 36-45; David Apter, "Some Reflections on the Role of a Political Opposition in New Nations," *Comparative Studies in Society and History*, 4 (1962), 154-68, esp. 154-58; Joseph La Palombara and Myron Weiner, eds., *Political Parties and Political Development*, (Princeton, N.J., 1966), 22-24, 203-4, 285, 296, 414-15. That party divisions were bad for the cause of Independence was noted by "An Undisguised Whig" in the *Pennsylvania Gazette*, Jan. 15, 1783.

14. An example of the "meshing" of party with the governing regime, one that also illustrates the way in which party communication between Philadelphia and the other counties was carried on, is a note from the secretary of the Philadelphia Constitutional Society to Joseph Reed, then president of the Supreme Executive Council, offering to circulate the resolves of the council to "our Bretheren in the Different Parts of this Commonwealth. . . ." Edward Pole to Joseph Reed, Mar. 28, 1779, Joseph Reed papers, New-York Historical Society. See also a letter from the Whig Society of Chester to Reed, Mar. 5, 1779, *ibid.* That party purposes often dictated the selection of the public printer in Pennsylvania

and that the press was an instrument of factional politics is noted by William Strahan in an undated letter to David Hall in "Notes and Queries," *Pennsylvania Magazine of History and Biography* 13 (1889), 484-85. Much of this was commonplace in pre-Revolutionary Pennsylvania. The Quaker and Proprietary factions of the 1750's and 1760's employed these techniques, but the Revolution intensified their use. See Gary B. Nash, "The Transformation of Urban Politics, 1700-1765," *Journal of American History,* 60 (1973), 605-32. George D. Rappaport has noted that a network of private associations of various sorts crisscrossed Pennsylvania and served as the functional equivalent of a party system. This "associational system" employed many of the techniques which we identify with early political parties. "Parties and Politics in Revolutionary Pennsylvania: An Institutional Analysis,' unpublished paper, 1976.

15. William N. Chambers, *Political Parties in a New Nation: The American Experience, 1776-1809* (New York, 1963), 19-21; Hofstadter, *Idea of a Party System,* 46; Jackson Turner Main, *Political Parties Before the Constitution* (Chapel Hill, N.C., 1973), 174.
16. J.H. Hutson, *Pennsylvania Politics, 1746-1770: The Movement for Royal Government and Its Consequences* (Princeton, N.J., 1972); Bonomi, "Middle Colonies," 74, 86n.
17. David Hawke, *In the Midst of a Revolution* (Philadelphia, 1961), 135-64.
18. Elisha P. Douglass, *Rebels and Democrats: The Struggle for Equal Political Rights and Majority Rule During the American Revolution* (Chicago, 1965), chap. 14.
19. Owen S. Ireland, "The Ratification of the Federal Constitution in Pennsylvania," (unpublished Ph.D. diss., University of Pittsburgh, 1966), 68-69. In the fall of 1776 a series of meetings of opponents of the new constitution took place in Philosophical Hall. Broadsides Ab 1776-2, 3, 4, Broadside Collection, Historical Society of Pennsylvania.
20. Ireland, "Ratification of the Constitution," 74 ff.
21. *Ibid.,* 106 ff.
22. *Pennsylvania Gazette,* Mar. 24, 1779.
23. Roland M. Baumann, "The Democratic-Republicans of Philadelphia: The Origins, 1776-1797," (unpublished Ph.D. diss., Pennsylvania State University, 1970), 19-21; Ireland, "Ratification of the Constitution," 24-27. The True Whigs were called "Furious Whigs" and "Yellow Whigs" by their enemies. See Brooke Hindle, *David Rittenhouse* (Princeton, N.J., 1964), 178-79; *Pennsylvania Gazette,* Mar. 24, 31, Apr. 9, 28, 1777.
24. Charles A. Beard, *An Economic Interpretation of the Constitution of the United States* (New York, 1948 ed.), 273-81; Robert L. Brunhouse, *The Counter-Revolution in Pennsylvania, 1776-1790* (Harrisburg, 1942); Douglass, *Rebels and Democrats,* chaps. 13-14; Orin G. Libby, *The Geographical Distribution of the Vote of the Thirteen States on the Federal Constitution, 1787-1788* (Madison, Wis., 1894), 26-29; Main, *Parties Before the Constitution,* xx, 24, 365-66.
25. Ireland, "Ratification of the Constitution," 6-7, 16-22, 70-73, *passim;* Baumann, "Democratic-Republicans," 12-13.
26. Wayne L. Bockelman and Owen S. Ireland, "The Internal Revolution in Pennsylvania: An Ethnic-Religious Interpretation," *Pennsylvania History,* 41 (1974), 125-59, quote on 127.
27. J.P. Nettl, *Political Mobilization: A Sociological Analysis of Methods and Concepts* (London, 1967), 139, 164, 170; Leon D. Epstein, "Political Par-

ties in Western Democratic Systems," in J.R. Hollingsworth, ed., *Nation and State Building in America: Comparative Historical Perspectives* (Boston, 1971), 205; Sigmund Neuman, "Toward a Comparative Study of Political Parties," in F.A. Bonadio, ed., *Political Parties in American History* (New York, 1974), II, 489.

28. La Palombara and Weiner, *Political Parties*, 13. In general, my discussion is based upon the first and last chapters of this work, supplemented by materials to be noted.

29. Ireland, "Ratification of the Constitution," 81.

30. "I need not point out to you the danger and folly of the [Pennsylvania] Constitution," Benjamin Rush wrote to Anthony Wayne. "It has substituted a mob government to one of the happiest governments in the world." To Charles Lee, he wrote, "Poor Pennsylvania! has become the most miserable spot upon the surface of the globe. Our streets have been stained already with fraternal blood [a reference to the Fort Wilson incident] — a sad prelude we fear of the future mischiefs our Constitution will bring upon us. They call it a democracy — a mobocracy in my opinion would be more proper. All our laws breathe the spirit of town meetings and porter shops." Rush to Wayne, May 19, 1777; Rush to Lee, Oct. 24, 1779, L.H. Butterfield, ed., *Letters of Benjamin Rush* (Princeton, N.J., 1951), I, 148, 244. Another observer called the constitution a "motley mixture of limited monarchy, and an execrable democracy — a Beast without a head" (quoted in Baumann, "Democratic-Republicans," 18). The Republican (anti-Constitutionalist) leaders, however, were men of moderate temperament who went along with the constitution even though they opposed its specific provisions. As one anti-Constitutionalist put it: "Our present government is lamentably defective, and has in it the seeds of the worst of tyrannies, but to attempt by force to overturn it, would, in my judgment, be wicked, as well as impolitic. The people who made it were fairly delegated for that purpose, and though they exceeded their power and acted wrong, yet it must be by persuasion and argument, not by force, that it must be altered." Edward Biddle to Clement Biddle, June 6, 1778, in William B. Reed, ed., *Life and Correspondence of Joseph Reed* (Philadelphia, 1847), 47n.

31. Circular letter of General Greene, Mar. 26, 1779, Joseph Reed Papers, New-York Historical Society.

32. Bockelman and Ireland, "Internal Revolution in Pennsylvania," esp. 127-33, 144-49. Benjamin Rush repeatedly referred to the overwhelming support of the Presbyterians for the Constitution, e.g., Rush to Anthony Wayne, May 19, 1777, *Rush Letters*, I, 148.

33. Bockelman and Ireland, "Internal Revolution in Pennsylvania," 142-43.

34. J.K. Martin, *Men in Rebellion: Higher Governmental Leaders and the Coming of the American Revolution* (New Brunswick, N.J., 1973), 44-45 (table and chart), *passim*,; Douglass, *Rebels and Democrats*, chap. 14. Benjamin Rush attributed the political polarization in Pennsylvania to these new men in politics, a number of whom were from out of state. "They see no old schoolmasters, no relations, no members of the same church or of the same clubs among those who are opposed to them to plead for charity and forbearance towards their errors or conduct, and hence their fury is unmixed and without bounds." Rush to John Montgomery, Nov. 5, 1782, *Rush Letters*, I, 292. Rush preferred old-boy elitism to the new politics.

35. Bockelman and Ireland, "Internal Revolution in Pennsylvania," 139. For the effects of the Revolutionary crisis on political participation in Pennsylvania, see R.A. Ryerson, *The Revolution is Now Begun: The Radical Committees of Philadelphia, 1765-1776* (Philadelphia, 1978).
36. Chilton Williamson, *American Suffrage: From Property to Democracy, 1760-1860* (Princeton, N.J., 1960), 92-97, 111-112, 133-34; Douglass, *Rebels and Democrats,* 251-52; Ireland, "Ratification of the Constitution," 280 (table); C.S. Olton, *Artisans for Independence: Philadelphia Mechanics and the American Revolution* (Syracuse, N.Y., 1975), chap. 8. One supporter of the Pennsylvania constitution argued that suffrage liberalization and the enlargement of the electorate was an effective way to "prevent corruption and party influence from operating in elections." *Pennsylvania Packet,* Dec. 5, 1778.
37. L.W. Pye and S. Verba, eds., *Political Culture and Political Development* (Studies in Political Development, Vol. 5; Princeton, N.J., 1965), 560; La Palombara and Weiner, *Political Parties,* 32-33, 430-31.
38. See J.T. Lemon and Gary B. Nash, "The Distribution of Wealth in Eighteenth-Century America: A Century of Change in Chester County, Pennsylvania, 1693-1802," *Journal of Social History,* 2 (1968), 1-24, who have concluded that in Chester County, at least, "the era of the American Revolution, far from reversing [the] creeping movement toward a consolidation of wealth and a deterioration in the economic position of the lower elements . . . only continued the trend and apparently accelerated it somewhat" (p. 14).
39. J.K. Alexander, "The Fort Wilson Incident of 1779: A Case Study of the Revolutionary Crowd," *William and Mary Quarterly,* 3rd ser., 31 (1974), 589-612.
40. For an illuminating discussion of the concept of political culture as a belief system, and one that I find has great applicability to Revolutionary Pennsylvania, see Pye and Verba, *Political Culture,* chap. 12.
41. What were thought to be the pernicious effects of party caused some members of the Continental Congress, which normally met in the same building as the Pennsylvania Assembly, to urge that it be relocated. "Congress have set too long in a City where every man effects the Politician, and having no system of his own, his Zeal is made subservient to the Designs of others, without his perceiving it. They must remove to some Spot where they will have a better chance to act independently." [Arthur Lee] to unknown [1783], in E.C. Burnett, ed., *Letters of Members of the Continental Congress* (Washington, 1921-36), VII, 106; also, Samuel Osgood to John Adams, Dec. 7, 1783, *ibid.,* 378; and see James Henderson, "Constitutionalists and Republicans in the Continental Congress, 1778-1786," *Pennsylvania History,* 36 (1969), 138.
42. Examples of anti-party statements in the Revolutionary press abound. See *Pennsylvania Gazette,* Feb. 24, 1779, where parties are referred to as "the dangerous diseases of civil freedom"; also, Sept. 22, 1779, Sept. 11, 1782, Jan. 15, Oct. 8, 1783, Jan. 21, Sept. 22, Dec. 8, 1784; *Pennsylvania Packet,* Oct. 15, 1776, Dec. 1, 1778; *Pennsylvania Journal,* Apr. 9, 1777, all of which contain aspersions against party and party spirit. In surveying the Pennsylvania press during these years, I have thus far found no major statement in support of the principle of party except for Franklin's remarks in his 1786 essay in *The American Museum.* At most, one finds a statement on the inevitability of party (*Independent Gazeteer,* Sept. 24,

1787), reference to the two Pennsylvania parties in a neutral and matter-of-fact way (*Pennsylvania Gazette*, Dec. 18, 1782), and the suggestion that parties actuated by patriotism are all right but to continue to support them once the constitution had been renewed was to act upon base and sordid motives (*Pennsylvania Gazette*, Dec. 8, 1784).

43. David Apter argues persuasively for the positive contribution opposi-tional politics can make in revolutionary regimes today. See "Some Reflections on the Role of Political Opposition," 158-68.

44. For an analysis of the substantive elements of colonial constitutionalism, see Dargo, *Roots of the Republic*, chaps. 3-6.

45. Stanley N. Katz, "The Politics of Law in Colonial America: Controversies over Chancery Courts and Equity Law in the Eighteenth Century," in *Law in American History*, D. Fleming and Bernard Bailyn, eds., *Perspectives in American History*, 5 (1971), 284. See also Jack P. Greene, *The Quest for Power: The Lower Houses of Assembly in the Southern Royal Colonies, 1689-1776* (New York, 1972 ed.), 9.

46. *American Magazine and Monthly Chronicle*, vol. I, no. 1, p. 34.

47. Thus I am differentiating colonial constitutionalism from modern con-stitutional theory which, in the words of one recent writer, "is deficient . . . in that it does not contain a concept of political action. It is a tradi-tion dedicated to the establishment of order even at the expense of action, and it fails to make adequate provision for innovative political activity at either the leadership or the participatory level." Kirk Thompson, "Con-stitutional Theory and Political Action," *Journal of Politics*, 31 (1969), 655.

48. Gordon S. Wood, *The Creation of the American Republic, 1776-1787* (Chapel Hill, N.C., 1969), parts 2-3. Not everyone agreed that the con-stitutional question deserved the priority it was receiving. Thus the New York delegation reported that in Pennsylvania "tho' the Enemy is daily expected an astonishing Langour prevails, and the embodying a compe-tent Force to oppose the meditated Invasion, seems to be a distant Object The Seat of this Disease is not an Indifference to the Cause . . . . The unhappy Dispute about their Constitution is the fatal Rock on which they have split and which threatens them with Destruction. We ardently wish that in our own State the utmost Caution may be used to avoid a like Calamity. Every wise Man here wishes that the Establishment of new Forms of Government had been deferred . . . ." Philip Livingston, James Duane, William Duer to Abraham Ten Broeck, Apr. 29, 1777, *Let-ters of the Continental Congress*, II, 344. Robert Morris reported to Horatio Gates on October 27, 1776, that the Maryland delegation was back home forming a constitution. "This seems to be the present business of all America, except the Army." *Ibid.*, 135. "*Constitutions* employ every pen . . . ." complained F.L. Lee to Landon Carter, Nov. 9, 1776, *ibid*, 149.

49. There was practically no serious discussion of political parties in political science literature prior to the Civil War. See Austin Ranney, "The Recep-tion of Political Parties into American Political Science," *Southwestern Social Science Quarterly*, 32 (1951), 183-91; Herman Belz, "The Constitu-tion in the Gilded Age: The Beginnings of Constitutional Realism in American Scholarship," *American Journal of Legal History*, 13 (1969), 110-25. For a different view, one which emphasizes the transforming ef-fect of the U.S. Constitution, "the end of classical politics," and the emergence of an "American Science of Politics" in the years immediately

following the enactment of the Federal Constitution, see Wood, *Creation of the American Republic*, chap. 15.

50. "The affair now in view is the most important that ever was before America. In my opinion it is the most important that has been transacted in any nation for some centuries past. If our civil Government is well constructed, and well managed, America bids fair to be the most glorious state that has ever been on earth. We should now at the beginning lay the foundation right. . . The plan of American Government, should, as much as possible, be formed to suit all the variety of circumstances that people may be in. . . . [F]or we may expect a variety of circumstances in a course of time, and we should be prepared for every condition." *Pennsylvania Packet*, July 1, 1776 (a reprint from a New York newspaper). For additional evidence of this attitude, see Wood, *Creation of the American Republic*, 127-32, *passim*. See also Douglass, *Rebels and Democrats*, 321.

51. On the distinction between *behavior* and *action*, see Thompson, "Constitutional Theory and Political Action," 661; see also Sheldon S. Wolin, *Politics and Vision: Continuity and Innovation in Western Political Thought* (Boston, 1960), 390-93.

52. For a defense of the constitutional formalism of the Framers, see Herman Belz, "New Left Reverberations in the Academy: The Antipluralist Critique of Constitutionalism," *Review of Politics*, 36 (1974), 265-83.

53. Wilson Carey McWilliams, "Civil Disobedience and Contemporary Constitutionalism," *Comparative Politics*, 1 (1969), 218.

54. Hofstadter, *Idea of a Party System*, chap. 2. "The Fathers hoped to create not a system of party government under a constitution but rather a constitutional government that would check and control parties" (p. 53). The Pennsylvania constitution of 1776 was criticized precisely because it promoted the growth of party by improving the chances of one party to control the unicameral legislature. "Let us abhor the idea of one party triumphing over the other, and generously unite to form such a model of government as may be beneficial to *all.*" *Pennsylvania Gazette*, Apr. 3, 1784.

55. Wolin's phrase (*Politics and Vision*, 414 ff), though used in a different connection.

56. Ranney, "The Reception of Political Parties," *passim*. Interestingly, the principle of press freedom seems to have survived the Revolution much better than the party principle. Thus "an undisguised Whig" excoriated party as divisive, damaging to the Revolutionary cause, and "a curse to the people," but, in equally vigorous terms, supported absolute freedom of the press: ". . . rather than the press should be under the least restraint by any power, it is more to the honor of government, and the happiness of the people, to suffer all the ribaldry, scurrility and bombast nonsense to be published, than that state rogues, villains, blood suckers and tyrants should eat up and destroy the people." *Pennsylvania Gazette*, Jan. 15, 1783. Another writer also differentiated between party distinctions and discords which had to be stopped, and a free press, the true "bulwark of freedom." *Ibid.*, Dec. 8, 1784. The *Freeman's Journal* proclaimed in its first number (Apr. 25, 1781) that "the freedom . . . of these states . . . must rise or fall with the freedom of the press." See also an article by "A Pennsylvanian," June 13, 1781, *ibid.* Homer L. Calkin, "Pamphlets and Public Opinion During the American Revolution," *Pennsylvania Magazine of History and Biography* 64 (1940), 22-42, also

stresses the great enthusiasm for the liberty of the press as a constitutional principle during the Revolutionary period (31-32).

57. Paine, "Dissertation on First Principles of Government," reprinted in Philip S. Foner, ed., *The Complete Writings of Thomas Paine* (New York, 1945), II, 588. Paine's writings are studded with anti-party material. A good example is from an article he wrote in the *Pennsylvania Gazette*, March 7, 1787: "Party knows no impulse but spirit, no prize but victory. It is blind to truth, and hardened against conviction. It seeks to justify error by perseverance, and denies to its own mind the operation of its own judgment. A man under the tyranny of party spirit is the greatest slave upon earth, for none but himself can deprive him of the freedom of thought." *Ibid.,* 433. In 1786 Paine's opposition to the proposed repeal of the charter of the Bank of North America, a party measure, led him to question the value of the unicameral legislature which he had always vigorously supported. See his "Dissertations on Government; the Affairs of the Bank; and Paper Money," in *ibid.,* 367 ff, esp. 409.

58. *Observations upon the Present Government of Pennsylvania in Four Letters to the People of Pennsylvania* (Philadelphia, 1777), 7.

59. *Ibid.,* 9. "The factions, seditions, and rebellions of republics arise wholly from the want of checks and balances and from [the] defect of equal representation." Rush to John Adams, July 21, 1789, *Rush Letters,* I, 522; "Order and tranquility appear to be the natural consequences of a well-balanced republic. . . ." *Information to Europeans Who Are Disposed to Migrate to the United States,* by Benjamin Rush, Apr. 16, 1790, in *ibid.,* 557.

60. Bingham to unknown, May 3, 1784, Gratz Collection, Historical Society of Pennsylvania. Bingham added: "And the Sooner we can effectually destroy the Spirit of Party in Republican Governments, the more we Shall promote the Happiness of Society . . . ."

61. On populist and conservative opposition to parties in new regimes, see Samuel P. Huntington, *Political Order in Changing Societies* (New Haven, 1968), 403.

62. Worthington C. Ford, ed., *Journals of the Continental Congress, 1774-1789* (Washington, 1904-37), IV, 342.

63. Hawke, *In the Midst of a Revolution,* 119-27.

Stephen E. Patterson (Pages 115-118)

1. This theme is expanded upon in Stephen E. Patterson, *Political Parties in Revolutionary Massachusetts* (Madison, Wis., 1973), chap. 1.

2. Hutchinson to Israel Williams, Apr. 26, 1765, Israel Williams Papers, II, 159, Massachusetts Historical Society.

3. John Adams and [Daniel Leonard], *Novanglus and Massachusettensis* (Boston, 1819), 149, 166.

4. At the Historical Society of Pennsylvania.

CONTRIBUTORS

PATRICIA U. BONOMI, a member of the department of history at New York University, is the author of *A Factious People: Politics and Society in Colonial New York* (1971) and an editor (with James MacGregor Burns and Austin Ranney) of *The American Constitutional System Under Strong and Weak Parties* (1980).

STEPHEN BOTEIN teaches history at Michigan State University. He is the author of " 'Meer Mechanics' and an Open Press: The Business and Political Strategies of Colonial American Printers," *Perspectives in American History*, 9 (1975).

DAVID R. CHESNUTT is Research Professor of History at the University of South Carolina and editor of *The Papers of Henry Laurens*. His research and publications have focused on South Carolina, Georgia, and East Florida in the pre-Revolutionary era.

GEORGE DARGO is on the history faculty at College of the Holy Cross. He is the author of *Jefferson's Louisiana: Politics and the Clash of Legal Traditions* (1975) and *Roots of the Republic: A New Perspective on Early American Constitutionalism* (1974).

MARC EGNAL teaches history at York University, Ontario. Among his writings is "The Politics of Ambition: A New Look at Benjamin Franklin's Career," *Canadian Review of American Studies*, VI (1975).

JOSEPH A. ERNST, a member of the history department at York University, Ontario, is the author of *Money and Politics in America, 1755-1775* (1973). He is currently writing a study to be titled "Essays in the Political Economy of Empire and Revolution."

STANLEY N. KATZ is Class of 1921 Bicentennial Professor of the History of American Law and Liberty at Princeton University. He is the author of *Newcastle's New York: Anglo-American Politics, 1732-1753* (1968).

ALISON GILBERT OLSON teaches history at the University of Maryland. She is the author of *Anglo-American Politics: Political Parties in England and Colonial America* (1973).

STEPHEN E. PATTERSON, a member of the history faculty at the University of New Brunswick, is the author of *Political Parties in Revolutionary Massachusetts* (1973).

J.G.A. POCOCK is a member of the history department at The Johns Hopkins University. He is the author of several books and essays, including *The Machiavellian Moment: Florentine Political Thought and the Atlantic Republican Tradition* (1975).

INDEX

Adams, John, 17, 113; as "Novanglus,"
22, 117
Adams, Randolph, G., 35, 37
Adams, Samuel, 22, 57, 59
Alexander, James, 55
Alexander family, 54
Allen, James, 57, 58
Allen, William, 51, 53
Allston, Joseph, 80
Americanization of the Common Law
(Nelson), 38
*American Revolution: A Constitutional
Interpretation* (McIlwain), 37
Andros, Gov. Edmund, 13, 22
Anglican faction (Pennsylvania), 53
Anne, Queen, 5, 6
Anti-Leislerian faction (New York), 46-47
Aristotle, 19

Bailyn, Bernard, 7-8, 36, 38
Baldwin, Alice Mary, 36
Bancroft, Edward, 30, 127
Barnard, Sir John, 64
Bayard, Nicholas, 46
Bayley, James, 40
Beard, Charles, 103, 117, 118
Becker, Carl, 35, 37
Bedford, Duke of (John Russell), 63, 65
Beekman, Gerard, 56
Beekman family, 48, 54, 56
Belcher, Jonathan, 50
Bellomont, Earl of, (Gov. Richard Coote),
46-47
Berkeley, Gov. William, 63
Bernard, Gov. Francis, 58-59, 75
Bingham, William, 112
Blackstone, Sir William, 39
Board of Trade, 62, 66, 83
Bolingbroke, Viscount (Henry St. John),
6, 7, 36, 72
Boone, Gov. Thomas, 71, 88-89
Bowdoin, James, 58
Bowdoin family, 56
Boyer, Paul, 40
Braddock, Gen. Edward, 52, 55

Brattle, Thomas, 48
Brown, Richard M., 87, 97
Bryan, George, 53
Bull, Lt. Gov. William, 73, 78-79, 80, 81,
89-90, 93, 95-96
Burke, Edmund, 14
Burlamaqui, Jean Jacques, 16
Burnet, Gov. William, 47, 50
Burroughs, George, 40

Calvin's Case, 19
Canty, Charles, 74
Chambers, William, 11
Charles II, King, 4
Charters, colonial, 30-32, 99, 108
Chauncy, Charles, 25, 27, 31
Choate, John, 57
Church, Benjamin, 13, 31
Churches: disestablishment of, 108; and
territorial expansion issue, 66, 67.
See also Clergy (New England);
Religion
Cicero, 19
Circuit Court Act of 1768 (South
Carolina), 72, 81, 83, 87, 92, 94;
revision of, 83, 87, 96-97
Civil War, English, 2-4, 41, 120
Clap, Thomas, 26-27
Clarke, Gov. George, 54-55
Clausewitz, Karl von, 3, 4
Cleaveland, John, 25, 26, 29, 32
Clergy (New England): Anglican, 27,
28, 30; Arminian, 25, 26, 27, 28, 29;
Calvinist, 26, 29, 32;
Congregationalist, 15, 27-28, 30; and
congregations, 24-26, 39-40; and
natural rights, 15-33 (passim), 122;
and Revolutionary movement, 15-33
(passim), 36-37, 122
Clinton, Gov. George, 54-55
Clymer, George, 53
Coffel, Joseph, 82, 95-96
Coke, Sir Edward, 14, 19, 39
Common law, 14, 16, 19, 23, 35, 39,
41-42, 99

151

Common Sense (Paine), 29
Commons House election of 1768 (South Carolina), xi, 70, 73-78, 87, 95
Constitution, English, 19, 22
Constitution, Pennsylvania, 100, 102-3, 105, 107, 115, 116, 117, 144, 146, 147
Constitution, U.S., 103, 115
Constitutionalism, 33-34, 98-100, 108-14, 115, 118, 146
Constitution Society (Pennsylvania), 103, 105, 106-8, 116
Continental Congress, Second, 113, 145.
Contractual rights, 21, 23-24, 29, 31, 39
Cooke, Elisha, Sr., 49
Cooke, Elisha, Jr., 49, 50
Cornbury, Viscount, Gov. (Edward Hyde), 47
Cortlandt Manor, 46
Cosby, Gov. William, 48
"County community" (England), 2-3, 4
Creation of the American Republic (Wood), 36
Cromwell, Oliver, 3
Cruger, John, 56
Cruger family, 54, 56
Cushing, Thomas, Sr., 57, 59

Dargo, George, 38
Dart, Benjamin, 76, 78
Davenant, Charles, 63
Davidson, Philip, 36
Debt Acts of 1714, 1717 (New York), 47
Declaration of Independence, 33, 125
Declaration of Independence (Becker), 35
Defence of the New-England Charters (Dummer), 30
Defense spending, as colonial issue, 48-50, 54-55, 58, 67
DeLancey, James, 48, 54-55, 56, 65, 66
DeLancey, Stephen, 47
DeLancey family, 54, 56
Democratic Republican party, 5, 11
DePeyster, Abraham, 46, 47
DePeyster family, 48
Dickinson, John, 53, 117
Dominion of New England, 22
Drayton, William Henry, 85, 97
Dudley, William, 50
Dulaney, Daniel, 69

Dummer, Jeremiah, 30, 31
Dummer, William, 50
Duverger, Maurice, 67

Eastern Association (England), 3
East Florida, 71, 86
Everitt, A.M., 2
Expansionists, *see* Territorial expansion

Faction, *see* Party and faction
Fairfax, Lord Thomas, 68
Faneuil, Benjamin, 58
Farrar, Benjamin, 74
Federalist party, 5, 11
Fisher, Joseph, 44
Fletcher, Gov. Benjamin, 46
Fort Wilson incident (1779), 107
France, colonial wars with, 44, 49, 50, 51, 52, 55-56, 106
Franchise, voting, 100; in Pennsylvania, 106-7, 145
Franklin, Benjamin, 51, 52, 53, 54, 101
Freer, John, 80
French and Indian War, 51, 52, 55-56, 106
Friends of Liberty, 59

Gadsden, Christopher, 71, 76, 77-78, 84, 89, 92, 140
Gadsden Election controversy (South Carolina), 71, 88
Gaillard, Tacitus, 73, 74, 79, 82
Gaillard, Theodore, 74
Garth, Charles, 72
Gay, Ebenezer, 25, 26, 28
"General Plan of Regulation" (Regulators), 72-73, 94
Gentry Whigs (South Carolina), 70-71, 77-78, 83, 84-85, 86
George I, King, 4
George III, King, 29
Georgia, x, 71, 86, 106
Glen, Gov. James, 71
Glorious Revolution, 5, 17, 41, 125
Glorious Revolution in America (Lovejoy), 41
Gordon, Gov. Patrick, 45-46
Gordon, Thomas, 36
Gouverneur family, 48
Grant, Col. James, 88
Great Awakening, 24, 26, 37, 66

Great Britain, *see* Party, English;
  Politics, English
Greene, Jack, P., 70
Greene, Gen. Nathaniel, 105

Hale, Robert, 57
Hamilton, Alexander, 11
Hamilton, Andrew, 45
Hamilton, James, 51
Hancock, John, 17, 59
Hancock, Thomas, 57, 58
Hancock family, 56, 59
Harrington, James, 17
Hartz, Louis B., 8
Heimert, Alan E., 37
Heyward, Daniel, 80
Hichborn, Benjamin, 34
Highland Patent, 46
Hillsborough, Lord (Wills Hill), 75, 78
History of Massachusetts-Bay
  (Hutchinson), 49
Hitchcock, Gad, 29
Hoadly, Benjamin, 17
Hofstadter, Richard, 11, 111
Holmes, Clive, 3
Holmes, Geoffrey, 5
Horwitz, Morton J., 38
Hovey, Ivory, 40
Hunter, Gov. Robert, 47
Hutcheson, Francis, 123
Hitchinson, Thomas, Sr., 49
Hutchinson, Gov. Thomas, 8, 49, 50, 58
  59, 116-17
Hutchinson family, 57, 59

*Ideological Origins of the American
  Revolution* (Bailyn), 36
Immigrant societies, colonial, 65-66
Imperial regulation, as colonial issue, 44,
  46, 47-48, 50-54, 55-56, 57-58, 61, 64,
  69; and English policy, 62-65
In a Defiant Stance... (Reid), 38
In a Rebellious Spirit... (Reid), 38
Independence, *see* Revolutionary
  movement
Indian relations, 47, 49-50, 64, 67, 71, 86
  88-89, 109
Ireland, 1

Jefferson, Thomas, 15, 123
Judicial review, 99, 129

Keith, Gov. William, 45-46
King George's War, 51, 52, 57, 58
King's College, 55
Kinsey, John, 51, 52
Kirkland, Moses, 74

Land riots, colonial, vii, 56
Langhorne, Jeremiah, 45
Laurens, Henry, 76, 77, 78, 79, 88, 89, 140
Law: common law, 14, 16, 19, 23, 35, 39,
  41-42, 99; historiography and, 14-15;
  judicial review, 99, 129; legal
  arguments in Revolutionary movement,
  14-16, 22-23, 28, 32, 37-38, 41, 108, 121;
  natural law, x, 15-34 (passim), 38,
  39-41, 115. 122, 124, 129
Lawyers, and Revolutionary movement,
  14, 28, 126
Legal Papers of John Adams (Wroth and
  Zobel), 38
Leisler, Jacob, 46
Leisler, Jacob, Jr., 47
Leislerian faction (New York), 46-48
Leonard, Daniel, as "Massachusettensis,"
  117
Libby, Orin, 117, 118
Lillie, Theophilus, 58
Livingston, Philip, 56
Livingston, Robert, 46, 47
Livingston family, 48, 54, 55, 56
Livingston Manor, 46, 47
Lloyd, David, 45
Lloyd, John, 77, 78
Lloyd, Thomas, 45
Locke, John, 15, 17, 27, 35, 36, 99,
  123, 125
Logan, James, 45
Loocock, Aaron, 74
Louisbourg, 52, 57, 58
Lovejoy, David S., 41
Lowndes, Rawlins, 80
Loyalists, x, 11, 44, 51, 53, 56, 68-69, 103,
  105, 107, 116-17
Loyalty test-oath law (Pennsylvania), 103,
  105, 106-7
Lynch, Thomas, 80, 84

McIlwain, Charles L., 37, 42
Mackenzie, John, 80, 84
Madison, James, 11, 101, 117-18
Magna Charta, 19, 30

Maine, 48, 49-50
Manchester, Earl of (Edward Montague), 3
Manigault, Peter, 75
Maryland, viii, 68
"Massachusettensis" (Daniel Leonard), 117
Massachusetts: defense spending, as issue in, 49, 50, 58; imperial regulation, as issue in, 57-58; money and currency, as issue in, 48, 49, 57, 58; party and faction in, x, 44, 48-50, 56-59, 116-117, 141-42; "Popular" party in, 50, 56, 57, 58, 59; "river gods," 57, 58, 59; territorial expansion, as issue in, 48-49, 56-59
Massachusetts Charter, 99
Massachusetts Circular Letter (1768), 74, 75, 78
Mather, Cotton, 24, 49
Mayhew, Jonathan, 24, 25, 26, 29, 37
Mease, John, 53
Mechanics party (South Carolina), 70, 72, 75-78, 84, 86
Mercantile associations, 66
Middleton, Col. Thomas, 88
Mifflin, Thomas, 53
Miller, Perry, 37
Milton, John, 16
Moderators (South Carolina), 82, 95-96
Mohawk Patent, 46
Money and currency, as colonial issue, 45-46, 48, 49, 57, 58, 61, 66, 67
Montagu, Gov. Charles, 79-80, 81, 82, 93, 95-96, 141
Morison, Samuel Eliot, 35
Morris, Anthony, 44, 45
Morris, Lewis, 47, 48
Morris, Robert, 51
Morrisania, 46
Morris family (New York), 54, 55, 56

Namier, Sir Lewis, 1-2, 5, 10
Natural law, x, 21-22, 23, 28, 31, 39-41, 115, 122, 124; and charter privileges, 30-32; historiography and, 15; and natural rights, 15-16, 21-22, 38; and Revolutionary movement, 15-16, 23, 38, 129

Natural rights, x, 15ff, 35-42 (passim), 128; and civil privileges, 20-21; and conscience, 20, 27, 28; and constitutionalism, 33-34; and contractual rights, 21, 23-24, 29, 31, 39; defined, 17-18; and natural law, 15-16, 21-22, 38; and property rights, 19-20, 28; and religion, x, 15-16, 18-19, 20, 26-27, 39; and Revolutionary movement, 15-33 (passim), 36, 128; and Scriptures, 18-19, 20
Nelson, William E., 38
Newcastle, Duke of (Thomas Pelham-Holles), 65
New England Clergy and the American Revolution (Baldwin), 36
New France, 47, 54
New York: defense spending, as issue in, 54-55; imperial regulation, as issue in, 47-48, 55-56; and inland trade, 47, 48, 54; land issue in, 46-47; Leislerians and anti-Leislerians in, 46-48; party and faction in, x, 44, 46-48, 54-56; territorial expansion, as issue in, 54-56
Nissenbaum, Stephen, 40
Non-expansionists, *see* Territorial expansion
Non-importation movement, 53, 75, 78, 80-82, 84
Norris, Isaac, 45, 51
North Carolina, viii
"Novanglus" (John Adams), 22, 117
Noyes, Oliver, 49, 50

Ohio territory, 51, 64
Oligarchy, age of, vi, ix, 5-6, 7, 8, 10, 12
Oliver, Peter, 15
Opposition politics, role of, vi, 7-8, 9-10, 11, 36, 99, 100-101
Oliver family, 57, 59
Otis, James, 16, 57, 58
Otis family, 59

Paine, Thomas, 29, 111-12, 148
Parliament, ix, 1-12 (passim), 30, 35
Parliament and the British Empire (Schuyler), 37
Parliamentarians (England), 4, 11
Parris, Samuel, 40

Parsons, James, 81
Party and faction: definitions of, 104, 119, 130, 136; historiography and, v-ix, 1, 43, 98, 103-4, 117, 146-47
Party, English, 1-12; historiography of, 1-3, 5-6, 10; opposition, 7-8, 9-10, 11. *See also* Politics, English
Patriots, x, 44, 51, 53-54, 56, 68-69
Patronage, political, vii, 1, 6, 8, 9, 11, 12, 55, 65, 86
Patterson, Stephen E., 69
Payne, William, 49
Pegues, Claudius, 74
Pemberton, Phineas, 44, 45
Penn, William, 45, 106
Pennsylvania: Assembly, 52, 105; constitution of, 100, 102-3, 105, 107, 115, 116, 117, 144, 146, 147; Constitution Society in, 103, 105, 106-8, 116; expansionists and non-expansionists in, 51-54; franchise, voting, in, 106-7, 145; imperial regulation, as issue in, 50-54; loyalty test-oath law in, 103, 105, 106-7; money and currency, as issue in, 45-46; party and faction in, x, xi, 44-46, 51-54, 102-14 (passim), 116-18, 142-43, 145-46; Proprietary faction in, 45, 52, 53, 116; Quaker factions in, 44-46, 52-53, 105-6, 116; religious factions in, 53, 106; Republican Society in, 103, 105, 108, 116, 144; Whig Society in, 103, 143
Pennsylvania Charter of Privileges, 99
Pennsylvania Provincial Conference, 102, 105-6
Philadelphia College, 103
Philipsborough, 46
Philipse, Adolph, 47
Philipse, Frederick, 46
Philipse family, 54, 56
Pinckney, Charles, 77, 78
Pinckney, Roger, 73
Pitt, William (1708-78), 7, 55
Plato, 19
Plumb, J.H., 5-6
Pocock, J.G.A., 63
Political Ideas of the American Revolution (Adams), 35
Politics, colonial, 8-9; historiography and, vi-ix; in New England, 13ff; and

opposition, role of, 99, 101; and patronage, vii, 8, 9, 12, 55, 86; structure of, vii-viii, 99-100; and territorial expansion, 61-62. *See also* Revolutionary movement; individual colonies
Politics, English, ix, 1-12; and connections, ix, 1-2, 4, 5-7, 8, 9; county (shire), ix, 1-2, 3, 6, 8-9, 10, 12; and imperial policy, 62-65; and patronage, 1, 6, 11, 12, 65. *See also* Party, English
"Popular" party (Massachusetts), 50, 56, 57, 58, 59
Pownall, Gov. Thomas, 58
Presbyterian faction (Pennsylvania), 53
Press, role of, 99, 108, 109, 147-48
Price, Hopkin, 76-77, 78
Privy Council, 66
Propaganda and the American Revolution (Davidson), 36
Property rights, 19-20, 28
Proprietary faction (Pennsylvania), 45, 52, 53, 116
Pufendorf, Baron Samuel von, 16
Puritanism, 15, 23, 27, 28, 36, 37, 125
Pusey, Caleb, 44, 45

Quaker Dissidents (Pennsylvania), 44-46
Quaker Grandees (Pennsylvania), 44-45
Quaker party (Pennsylvania), 52-53, 116
Quebec Act, 64
Quitrents, 45

Rawle, Francis, 45
Redman, Joseph, 44
Regulators (South Carolina), xi, 70-97 (passim); and Circuit Court Act of 1768, 72, 83, 87, 92, 96-97; and Commons House election of 1768, 70, 73-74, 95; and "General Plan of Regulation," 72-73, 94; march on Charleston, threat by, 73-74, 81, 87; and Moderators, 82, 95-96; origins of, 72-73, 88-91; and "Remonstrance," 93-94
Reid, John Phillip, 38
Religion, and natural rights, x, 15-16, 18-19, 20, 26-27, 39. *See also* Churches; Clergy, (New England);

Puritanism

Religion and the American Mind from the Great Awakening to the Revolution (Heimert), 37

"Remonstrance" (Regulators), 93-94

Republican (Democratic Republican) party, 5, 11

Republican Society (Pennsylvania), 103, 105, 108, 116, 144

Restoration (England), 5

Revolution, American, interpretations of, v-vi. *See also* Revolutionary movement

Revolutionary movement, 9, 10; and charter privileges, 30-32; and clergy, 15-33 (passim), 36-37, 39-40, 122; historiography of, 7-8, 14-15, 35-39, 118; lawyers and, 14, 28, 126; legal arguments and, 14-16, 22-23, 28, 32, 37-38, 41, 108, 121; and natural rights theory, x, 15-33 (passim), 36, 128; non-importation and, 53, 75, 78, 80-82, 84; and opposition politics, vi, 36, 99, 100-101; and territorial expansion issue, 53, 56, 59-60. *See also* Politics, colonial

Rhode Island, viii

"River gods" (Massachusetts), 57, 58, 59

Robbins, Caroline, 36

Roberdeau, Robert, 53, 54

Robinson, Patrick, 44

Roots of the Republic: A New Perspective on Early American Constitutionalism (Dargo), 38

Royalists (England), 4, 11

Rush, Benjamin, 112

Savage, Thomas, 76, 78

Schuyler, Peter, 47

Schuyler, Philip, 47

Schuyler, Robert Livingston, 37

Scotland, 1

Secker, Archbishop Thomas, 27

Septennial Act (England), 5

Seven years' War, 64

Sewall, Samuel, 49

Shebbeare, John, 64

Shinner, Chief Justice Charles, 72, 80, 89, 92-93

Shirley, Gov. William, 55, 57, 65, 66

Shute, Gov. Samuel, 49

Sidney, Algernon, 17

Sinker, Peter, 80

Sirmans, Eugene M., 70

Slaves and slavery, 71, 76

Smith, Benjamin, 84

Smith, Thomas, Sr., 76

Smith, Thomas, of Broad Street, 76

Smith, William, Sr., 55

Smith, William, 101, 109-10

Somers, Lord John, 17

Sons of Liberty, 20

Sources and Documents Illustrating the American Revolution, 1764-1788 (Morison), 35

South Carolina: Commons House election of 1768, xi, 70, 73-78, 87, 95; Gentry Whigs in, 70-71, 77-78, 83, 84-85, 86; mechanics party in, 70, 72, 75-78, 84, 86; Moderators in, 82, 95-96; and non-importation, 75, 78, 80-82, 84; party and faction in, x-xi, 70ff; Regulators in, xi, 70-97 (passim)

Spain, colonial war with, 44, 50, 52

Speck, W.A., 5

Staats, Samuel, 46, 47

Stamp Act (1765), 14, 28, 77, 84, 89, 93

Swift, Joseph, 53

Tennent, William, 97

Territorial expansion, as colonial issue, 44-60 (passim), 61-62, 65-69; as imperial issue, 61-69

Thomas, Gov. George, 52

Thompson, William, 74

Thomson, Charles, 53

Timothy, Peter, 73, 74, 88, 90

Tories, *see* Loyalists

Tory party (England), 2, 4-5, 6-7, 11

Townshend, Penn, 48

Townshend Acts duties, 70, 74, 75-76, 78, 80-82

Trade, inland, 47, 48, 54, 71

Transformation of American Law, 1780-1860 (Horwitz), 38

Trenchard, John, 36

Turner, Robert, 44

Tyng, John, 57, 58

Van Cortlandt family, 54

Van Rennsselaer family, 48, 54

Vattel, Emmerich von, 16

Virginia, x, 63, 68
Virginia Circular Letter (1768), 81
Voting, *see* Franchise

Walcott, Robert R., 5
Walpole, Horace, 6, 7, 11
Walters, Robert, 47
Walton family, 54
Ward, John, 77
Washington, George, 33
Weir, Robert M., 70, 87, 97
Wells, Robert, 88
Wharton, Thomas, 117
Whig party (England), 2, 4-5, 6-7, 11, 12, 65

Whigs, Gentry (South Carolina), 70-71, 77-78, 83, 84-85, 86
Whig Society (Pennsylvania), 103, 143
Wilkes, John, 7
Wilkes Fund controversy, 71
Williams, Elisha, 27
Willing, Thomas, 51, 53, 54
Winthrop, Wait, 48
Wood, Gordon S., 36, 38, 41
Woodmason, Charles, 82, 92, 93-94
Wragg, William, 80, 88, 89, 94
Wroth, Kinvin, 38

Zenger, John Peter, 48
Zobel, Hiller, 38

Books of Interest
by
The Sleepy Hollow Press

An Emerging Independent American Economy: 1815-1875

edited by Joseph R. Frese, S.J. and Jacob Judd

Distinguished scholars discuss the importance of transporation, technology, and entrepreneurial skills in establishing an independent economy in nineteenth-century America.

224 pages, notes, index, ISBN 0-912882-40-9   cloth, $20.00

Life Along the Hudson

by Allan Keller

Illustrated history of the Hudson River Valley, drawing on legend and fact for a unique perspective.

272 pages, illus., bibliog., index. ISBN 0-912882-20-4   cloth, $10.00

Life of George Washington

edited and abridged by Jess Stein

The classic biography adapted for the modern reader, with an introduction by Richard B. Morris.

800 pages, illus., chronology, index, ISBN 0-912882-18-2   cloth, $19.95

For information and our free catalog, write:

**The Sleepy Hollow Press
150 White Plains Road
Tarrytown, New York 10591**

Books of Interest
by
The Sleepy Hollow Press

The Loyalist Americans

edited by Robert East and Jacob Judd

Essays exploring the significance of Americans who remained loyal to the British Crown during the Revolutionary War.

192 pages, illus., bibliog., index, ISBN 0-912882-14-X   cloth, $12.00

The Mill
at Philipsburg Manor, Upper Mills, and
A Brief History of Milling

by Charles Howell and Allan Keller

A study of milling technology, emphasizing the reconstructed gristmill at Philipsburg Manor, Upper Mills.

192 pages, illus., bibliog., glossary, index, ISBN 0-912882-22-0 cloth, $15.00

For information and our free catalog, write:

The Sleepy Hollow Press
150 White Plains Road
Tarrytown, New York 10591